THE PIE MAKER

THE AUSTRALIAN Women's Weekly

The PIE MAKER

CONTENTS

EASY AS PIE 6

PIE TIME 8

SWEET AS PIE 50

SWEET STUFF 94

THE OTHER STUFF 142

GLOSSARY 184

CONVERSION CHART 188

INDEX 189

EASY AS PIE

Australians have always had a love affair with pies, so much so, that there might even been an argument to claim them as our national dish. Up until now, the only thing standing in the way of creating a decent pie for many cooks, was the sizeable chunk of time required to make them, and a fear of failure.

The real game changer for the pie-loving cook, aside from the accessibility of good-quality ready-made pastry sheets, is the proliferation of affordable pie-making machines. These nifty devices are failsafe and fast, efficiently browning both the top and bottom of the pie equally to crisp perfection. In short, with a pie maker, pies can be whipped up at whim, putting pie-making success within reach of every cook. And the fun doesn't end just with making pies. These little gems of convenience will cook all sorts of ingenious snacks or 'other stuff'. There are tasty sweet and savoury creations great for breakfast, lunch box treats and dessert. Even another national favourite – mini pavlovas – all are possibilities in a pie maker.

SIZE MATTERS Most brands of pie makers are designed to make four individual pies and are similar to operate. The main difference between brands lies in the size of the pies they make. One of the most popular-sized machine makes ⅓-cup (80ml) pies, however there are also machines for larger ¾-cup (180ml) pies, and even those that produce a single 2½-cup (625ml) family-sized pie.

The majority of the recipes in this book are for a 4-hole (⅓-cup/80ml) pie maker, but there are several meat pie recipes designed for a 4-hole (¾-cup/180ml) pie maker, plus a sprinkling of sweet and savoury options for family-sized pies. Regardless of the machine you have, once you know the capacity of each hole, you can adapt the amount of filling you need for your particular machine. Alternatively, simply aim to always leave a 2mm (¹⁄₁₂in) gap between the top of the filling and the rim of the pastry before cooking a tart, or covering with pastry for a pie, unless otherwise specified in a recipe. Before you start making any recipes in this book, determine the capacity of the individual holes of your pie maker. To do this, fill a small measuring cup with water and fill a pie hole to the brim. As a guide, these are the hole capacities for the three most common machines:

4-hole (⅓-cup/80ml) each hole will hold approximately ¼ cup filling.
4-hole (¾-cup/180ml) each hole will hold approximately ⅔ cup filling.
family-sized single pie holds approximately 2⅓ cups filling.

Take care not to over fill your pies or they will make a mess. You can always check one pie before filling them all. It is also important to read your pie makers' instruction manual for further specific guidance around use.

UTENSILS Your pie maker has a non-stick coating, which is best preserved by using non-stick cooking utensils. Most pie makers come equipped with a cutter designed to cut out both the bottom and top rounds of pastry to fit the brand of pie maker. However, each of our recipes also notes the size of the pastry rounds required.

CLEANING When making multiple batches of pies, wipe the pie holes clean with a damp piece of paper towel and avoid the use of abrasive cleaning agents.

PASTRY The best combination for most pies (or for tart bases) is a shortcrust base for crispness and then either a puff pastry or shortcrust top. For speed, pastry rounds can be cut to size and stored in the freezer so you have them on hand. You can also use the pie maker to make tart shells, see page 93.

PREPPING Meat pie fillings can all be made ahead and refrigerated. They also freeze well. To reheat frozen pies, place ⅓-cup (80ml) pies in the pie maker for 14 minutes and ¾-cup (180ml) pies for 12 minutes. (Note that the pastry will continue to brown.) Alternatively, reheat in a 180°C/350°F oven for 15 minutes.

HOLDING THE MACHINE LID AJAR. Use a heatproof object, such as a wooden spoon or a narrow roll of paper towel as a wedge at the front of the machine to prevent the lid from squashing the contents.

> **LUNCH BOX FILLERS, BREAKFAST, SWEET AND SAVOURY TREATS ARE ALL POSSIBILITIES IN A PIE MAKER.**

PIE TIME

SMOKY CHICKEN & CORN PIES

PREP + COOK TIME 12 MINUTES
MAKES 4

ingredients

1 sheet frozen shortcrust pastry, thawed
1 sheet frozen puff pastry, thawed
⅔ cup (120g) shredded barbecue chicken
½ cup (120g) sour cream
8 slices chorizo (40g), chopped coarsely
¼ cup (50g) canned corn kernels, plus extra to serve (optional)
2 tablespoons thinly sliced green onion (scallion)
1 egg, beaten lightly
⅓ cup (80g) sour cream, extra
2 teaspoons Tabasco chipotle sauce

1 Lightly grease and preheat a 4-hole (⅓-cup/80ml) pie maker.

2 Using pastry cutter provided, cut four large rounds (11cm/4½in) from shortcrust pastry and four small rounds (9.5cm/4in) from puff pastry. Line prepared holes with shortcrust pastry rounds, pressing into base and side.

3 Divide shredded chicken, sour cream, chorizo, corn and 1 tablespoon of the green onion among pastry cases. Top with puff pastry rounds; press edges firmly to seal. Brush pastry with egg. Close lid; cook pies for 7 minutes or until browned.

4 Serve pies topped with extra sour cream, extra corn, Tabasco chipotle sauce and remaining green onion.

TURKEY & CRANBERRY PIES

PREP + COOK TIME 12 MINUTES MAKES 4

ingredients

1 sheet frozen shortcrust pastry, thawed

1 sheet frozen puff pastry, thawed

100g (3oz) shaved roast turkey breast

140g (4½oz) brie, chopped coarsely

⅓ cup (100g) cranberry sauce, plus extra to serve

1 egg, beaten lightly

1 Lightly grease and preheat a 4-hole (⅓-cup/80ml) pie maker.

2 Using pastry cutter provided, cut four large rounds (11cm/4½in) from shortcrust pastry and four small rounds (9.5cm/4in) from puff pastry. Line prepared holes with shortcrust pastry rounds, pressing into base and side.

3 Divide turkey, brie and cranberry sauce among pie cases. Top with puff pastry rounds; press edges firmly to seal. Brush pastry with egg. Close lid; cook pies for 7 minutes or until browned.

4 Serve pies straightaway with extra cranberry sauce.

pie time

BACON & EGG PIES

PREP + COOK TIME 12 MINUTES
MAKES 4

ingredients

1 sheet frozen shortcrust pastry, thawed
1 sheet frozen puff pastry, thawed
4 eggs, straight from the fridge
60g (2oz) finely chopped bacon
1 egg, extra, beaten lightly
tomato sauce (ketchup), to serve

1 Lightly grease and preheat a 4-hole (⅓-cup/80ml) pie maker.

2 Using pastry cutter provided, cut four large rounds (11cm/4½in) from shortcrust pastry and four small rounds (9.5cm/4in) from puff pastry. Line prepared holes with shortcrust pastry rounds, pressing into base and side.

3 Crack an egg into each pie case, being careful not to over fill, leaving a 2mm (1/12in) gap for the bacon. Divide bacon on top; season with pepper. Top with puff pastry rounds; press edges firmly to seal. Brush pastry with extra egg. Close lid; cook pies for 7 minutes or until browned.

4 Serve pies straightaway with tomato sauce.

tip For a vegetarian version, replace bacon with 4 slices of tomato and 2 teaspoons soft goat's cheese.

SMOKED OCEAN TROUT & WASABI PIES

PREP + COOK TIME 20 MINUTES (+ STANDING) MAKES 4

ingredients

375g (12oz) frozen peas
2 tablespoons butter
2 teaspoons lime juice
1 sheet frozen shortcrust pastry, thawed
1 sheet frozen puff pastry, thawed
150g (4½oz) smoked ocean trout fillet, flaked
1 egg, beaten lightly

WASABI CREAM

½ cup (120g) crème fraîche
2 teaspoons lime juice
¾ teaspoon wasabi paste

1 To make wasabi cream, combine crème fraîche, lime juice and wasabi in a small bowl.

2 Place frozen peas in a heatproof bowl, pour over boiling water; stand for 1 minute, then drain. Puree peas, butter and lime juice, using a stick blender. Season to taste.

3 Lightly grease and preheat a 4-hole (⅓-cup/80ml) pie maker.

4 Using pastry cutter provided, cut four large rounds (11cm/4½in) from shortcrust pastry and four small rounds (9.5cm/4in) from puff pastry. Line prepared holes with shortcrust pastry rounds, pressing into base and side.

5 Spread 1 tablespoon mushy peas into each pie case, divide evenly with flaked trout, then top each with 2 teaspoons of the wasabi cream. Top with puff pastry rounds; press edges firmly to seal. Brush pastry with egg. Close lid; cook pies for 7 minutes or until browned.

6 Serve pies topped with remaining mushy peas and wasabi cream.

MUSHROOM PIES

PREP + COOK TIME 20 MINUTES MAKES 4

ingredients

cooking oil spray
4 white flat mushrooms (200g)
1 sheet frozen shortcrust pastry, thawed
⅓ cup (100g) caramelised onion
100g (3oz) marinated goat's cheese, crumbled
1 teaspoon fresh thyme leaves
4 fresh thyme sprigs
flaked salt, to serve

1 Preheat a 4-hole (⅓-cup/80ml) pie maker.

2 Spray holes with oil and place mushrooms, stalks facing up, into holes. Close lid; cook for 5 minutes or until softened. Remove mushrooms; drain on paper towel. Wipe holes clean with paper towel.

3 Using pastry cutter provided, cut four large rounds (11cm/4½in) from shortcrust pastry. Line prepared holes with shortcrust pastry rounds, pressing into base and side.

4 Spread 1 tablespoon caramelised onion into each pastry case, top with goat's cheese and thyme divided equally; season with pepper. Top with a whole mushroom, stalk-side down then thyme sprigs. Close lid; cook pies for 5 minutes or until browned.

5 Serve pies straightaway topped with salt.

BEEF TACO PIES

PREP + COOK TIME 55 MINUTES (+ COOLING)
MAKES 10

ingredients

10 x 15cm (6in) white corn tortillas
1 cup (120g) grated cheddar
1 cup (80g) shredded red cabbage
1 medium tomato (150g), chopped
½ cup (120g) guacamole
½ cup (120g) sour cream
coriander (cilantro) leaves and lime wedges, to serve

TACO FILLING

1 tablespoon olive oil
1 small onion (80g), chopped finely
1 clove garlic, crushed
500g (1lb) minced (ground) beef
30g (1oz) packet taco seasoning mix
400g (12½oz) can diced tomatoes
2 tablespoons tomato paste
⅓ cup (80ml) beef stock

1 To make taco filling, heat oil in a large frying pan; cook onion and garlic, stirring, until onion softens. Add beef; cook, stirring to break up lumps with the back of a spoon, for 5 minutes or until browned. Stir in seasoning mix, tomatoes, paste and stock; bring to the boil. Reduce heat; simmer, for 15 minutes or until thickened. Season to taste. Cool. (Makes 3½ cups.)

2 Lightly grease and preheat a 4-hole (¾-cup/180ml) pie maker (see tips). Wrap tortillas in paper towel; reheat in the microwave on HIGH (100%) for 40 seconds. Keep warm in a clean tea towel. (Heating the tortillas will make them more pliable and prevents them from tearing.) Line prepared holes with tortillas, pressing into base and side.

3 Spoon ⅓ cup taco filling and 1 tablespoon cheese into each tortilla case. Close lid; cook for 8 minutes or until cheese is golden. Remove taco pies; transfer to a wire rack. Repeat with remaining tortillas and taco filling to make 10 in total.

4 Top pies with cabbage, tomato, guacamole and sour cream. Serve with coriander and lime wedges.

tips To make these in a smaller pie maker, see page 7 for information on how much filling they hold, then adjust accordingly. You can also use larger tortillas and cut to size using the pastry cutter provided. If you like a kick to your tacos, add a pinch of chilli flakes. The taco filling will keep frozen for up to 3 months. Thaw in fridge overnight before using.

pie time

VEGAN CAULIFLOWER CHEEZE PIES

PREP + COOK TIME 50 MINUTES
MAKES 4

ingredients

1 sheet frozen puff pastry, thawed
150g (4½oz) small cauliflower florets (see tips)
2 teaspoons extra virgin olive oil
1 large desiree potato (300g), peeled, grated coarsely

CHEEZE SAUCE
2 tablespoons extra virgin olive oil
1½ tablespoons plain flour (all-purpose flour)
1½ cups (375ml) almond milk
1½ tablespoons nutritional yeast
1½ teaspoons onion powder
½ teaspoon ground nutmeg

1 Preheat a 4-hole (⅓-cup/80ml) pie maker. Using pastry cutter provided, cut four small rounds (9.5cm/4in) from puff pastry. Refrigerate rounds until required.

2 Toss cauliflower in oil. Divide among holes; season with salt and pepper. Close lid; cook for 7 minutes. Turn florets. Close lid; cook for a further 5 minutes or until tender and edges brown. Remove cauliflower; drain on paper towel. Wipe holes clean with paper towel.

3 Meanwhile, to make cheeze sauce, heat oil in a small saucepan over medium heat, add flour; cook, until mixture bubbles and thickens. Gradually add milk, whisking until sauce boils and thickens. Remove from heat; stir in remaining ingredients and season to taste.

4 Place grated potato in a colander; squeeze firmly to remove as much moisture as possible. Combine grated potato and 2 tablespoons of cheeze sauce.

5 Spray pie maker holes generously with oil. Place 2 tablespoons potato mixture into each hole; press firmly into base and side, using the back of a spoon. Close lid; cook for 7 minutes. Gently turn potato cases over. Close lid; cook for a further 5 minutes or until golden brown.

6 Combine cauliflower florets with ¾ cup cheeze sauce; divide among potato cases. Top with pastry rounds (see tips); press edges firmly to seal. Spray tops of pies with oil. Close lid; cook pies for 7 minutes or until browned.

7 Serve pies with remaining sauce.

tips Cut cauliflower into very small florets so it cooks quickly. You can decorate the pies as pictured using the puff pastry scraps.

AUSSIE MEAT PIES

PREP + COOK TIME 1 HOUR (+ COOLING) MAKES 12

ingredients

3 sheets frozen shortcrust pastry
3 sheets frozen puff pastry, thawed
1 egg, beaten lightly
2 teaspoons sesame seeds
tomato sauce (ketchup), to serve

BEEF FILLING

1 tablespoon olive oil
1 small onion (80g), chopped finely
1 clove garlic, crushed
500g (1lb) minced (ground) beef
400g (12½oz) can diced tomatoes
2 tablespoons tomato paste
2 tablespoons worcestershire sauce
½ cup (125ml) beef stock

1 To make beef filling, heat oil in a large saucepan; cook onion, garlic and beef, stirring to break up lumps with back of a spoon, for 5 minutes or until beef is well browned. Stir in tomatoes, paste, sauce and stock; bring to the boil. Reduce heat; simmer, for 20 minutes or until thickened. Season to taste. Cool. (Makes 3 cups.)

2 Lightly grease and preheat a 4-hole (⅓-cup/80ml) pie maker.

3 Using pastry cutter provided, cut 12 large rounds (11cm/4½in) from shortcrust pastry and 12 small rounds (9.5cm/4in) from puff pastry. Line prepared holes with shortcrust pastry rounds, pressing into base and side. Refrigerate remaining pastry rounds until required.

4 Spoon ¼ cup beef filling into each pie case. Top with puff pastry rounds; press edges firmly to seal. Brush pastry with egg. Sprinkle with sesame seeds. Close lid; cook pies for 8 minutes or until pastry is golden. Remove pies; transfer to a wire rack. Repeat with remaining pastry rounds, beef filling, egg wash and sesame seeds to make 12 pies in total.

5 Serve pies with tomato sauce.

tip Pies and beef filling will keep frozen for up to 3 months. Thaw in fridge overnight. Reheat pies in pie maker for 7 minutes.

PUB-STYLE GUINNESS BEEF PIES

PREP + COOK TIME 1 HOUR (+ COOLING)
MAKES 6

ingredients

6 sheets frozen shortcrust pastry, thawed
2 sheets frozen puff pastry, thawed
1 egg, beaten lightly
potato mash and gravy, to serve

BEEF FILLING
2 cloves garlic
2 teaspoons fresh rosemary
1 small onion (80g)
1 stalk celery (150g)
1 medium carrot (120g)
3 portobello mushrooms (150g)
750g (1½lb) beef eye fillet steak
1 tablespoon olive oil
1 tablespoon plain flour (all-purpose flour)
1 cup (250ml) Guinness
½ cup (125ml) beef stock

1 To make beef filling, finely chop garlic, rosemary and vegetables. Cut beef into 3cm (1¼in) pieces. Heat half the oil in a large heavy-based saucepan over high heat; cook beef in batches, until browned. Transfer to a plate. Heat remaining oil in same pan; cook garlic, rosemary and vegetables until softened. Stir in resting juices from beef then flour until mixture bubbles. Add Guinness and stock; bring to the boil. Reduce heat; simmer, covered, for 10 minutes. Remove lid; simmer for 5 minutes or until sauce thickens. Add browned beef; cook, uncovered, for 1 minute. Season. Cool. (Makes 4 cups.)

2 Lightly grease and preheat a 4-hole (¾-cup/180ml) pie maker.

3 Using pastry cutter provided, cut six large rounds (15.5cm/6¼in) from shortcrust pastry and six small rounds (12cm/4¾in) from puff pastry. Line prepared holes with shortcrust pastry rounds, pressing into base and side. Refrigerate remaining pastry rounds until required.

4 Spoon ⅔ cup beef filling into each pie case. Top with puff pastry rounds; press edges firmly to seal. Brush pastry with egg. Close lid; cook pies for 9 minutes or until pastry is golden. Remove pies; transfer to a wire rack. Repeat with remaining pastry rounds, beef filling and egg wash to make 6 pies in total.

5 Serve pies topped with mashed potato, leftover filling and gravy.

tips To make these in a smaller pie maker, see page 7 for information on how much filling they hold, then adjust accordingly. Pies and beef filling will keep for up to 3 months in airtight containers in the freezer. Thaw in fridge overnight. Reheat pies in pie maker for 11 minutes.

BEEF SHIRAZ PIES

PREP + COOK TIME 1 HOUR 30 MINUTES (+ COOLING) MAKES 6

ingredients

6 sheets frozen shortcrust pastry, thawed
2 sheets puff pastry, thawed
1 egg, beaten lightly
1 teaspoon fresh thyme leaves

BEEF SHIRAZ FILLING

1 medium onion (150g)
1 medium carrot (120g)
2 stalks celery (300g), trimmed
2 cloves garlic
650g (1¼lb) beef eye fillet steak
2 tablespoons olive oil
1 tablespoons plain flour (all-purpose flour)
½ cup (125ml) dry red wine (such as shiraz)
½ cup (125ml) beef stock
400g (12½oz) can diced tomatoes
2 tablespoons fresh thyme leaves

1 To make beef shiraz filling, finely chop vegetables and garlic. Cut steak into 3cm (1¼in) pieces. Heat half the oil in a large heavy-based saucepan over high heat; cook beef, in batches, until browned. Transfer to a plate. Heat remaining oil in same pan; cook chopped vegetables and garlic, stirring until softened. Stir in resting juices from beef, then flour until mixture bubbles. Add wine, stock, tomatoes and thyme; bring to the boil. Reduce heat; simmer, covered, for 10 minutes. Remove lid; simmer for 5 minutes or until thick and vegetables are tender. Add cooked beef; simmer, uncovered, for 1 minute. Season to taste. Cool. (Makes 4 cups.)

2 Lightly grease and preheat a 4-hole (¾-cup/180ml) pie maker.

3 Using pastry cutter provided, cut six large rounds (15.5cm/6¼in) from shortcrust pastry and six small rounds (12cm/4¾in) from puff pastry. Line prepared holes with shortcrust pastry rounds, pressing into base and side. Refrigerate remaining pastry rounds until required.

4 Spoon ⅔ cup beef filling into each pie case. Top with puff pastry rounds; press edges firmly to seal. Brush pastry with egg; sprinkle with thyme. Close lid; cook pies for 8 minutes or until pastry is golden. Remove pies; transfer to a wire rack. Repeat with remaining pastry rounds, beef filling, egg wash and thyme to make 6 pies in total.

tips To make these in a smaller pie maker, see page 7 for information on how much filling they hold, then adjust accordingly. Pies and beef filling will keep frozen for up to 3 months. Thaw in fridge overnight. Reheat the pies in pie maker for 12 minutes.

pie time

THAI CHICKEN CURRY PIES

PREP + COOK TIME 45 MINUTES (+ COOLING) MAKES 6

ingredients

6 sheets frozen shortcrust pastry, thawed
2 sheets frozen puff pastry, thawed
1 egg, beaten lightly

CURRY FILLING

1 tablespoon peanut oil
1 medium onion (150g), sliced thinly
⅓ cup (100g) thai green curry paste
800g (1½lb) chicken thigh fillets, cut into 2cm (¾in) pieces
100g (3oz) green beans, trimmed, chopped coarsely
3 kaffir lime leaves, torn (optional)
1 cup (250ml) coconut cream
1 tablespoon fish sauce
2 teaspoons cornflour (cornstarch)

1 To make curry filling, heat oil in a large saucepan; cook onion, stirring, until softened. Add curry paste and chicken; cook until browned. Stir in beans, lime leaves and coconut cream; bring to the boil. Reduce heat; stir in fish sauce. Simmer, for 10 minutes or until chicken is cooked and beans tender. Mix cornflour with 2 teaspoons water. Stir cornflour mixture into curry; simmer until mixture thickens. Season to taste. Cool. Discard lime leaves. (Makes 4½ cups.)

2 Lightly grease and preheat a 4-hole (¾-cup/180ml) pie maker.

3 Using pastry cutter provided, cut six large rounds (15.5cm/6¼in) from shortcrust pastry and six small rounds (12cm/4¾in) from puff pastry. Line prepared holes with shortcrust pastry rounds, pressing into base and side. Refrigerate remaining pastry rounds until required.

4 Spoon ⅔ cup curry filling into each pie case. Top with puff pastry rounds; press edges firmly to seal. Brush pastry with egg. Close lid; cook for 8 minutes or until pastry is golden. Remove pies; transfer to a wire rack. Repeat with remaining pastry rounds, curry filling and egg wash to make 6 pies in total.

tips To make these in a smaller pie maker, see page 7 for information on how much filling they hold, then adjust accordingly. Pies and curry filling will keep frozen for up to 3 months. Thaw in fridge overnight. Reheat pies in the pie maker for 12 minutes.

MOROCCAN LAMB PIES

**PREP + COOK TIME 1 HOUR 15 MINUTES (+ COOLING)
MAKES 6**

ingredients

6 sheets frozen shortcrust pastry, thawed

2 sheets frozen puff pastry, thawed

1 egg, beaten lightly

1 teaspoon cumin seeds

¾ cup (200g) greek yoghurt

1½ tablespoons harissa

LAMB FILING

1 small onion (80g)

1 medium carrot (140g)

1 clove garlic

600g (1¼lb) lamb loin

2 tablespoons olive oil

1 teaspoon each ground coriander, ground cinnamon, ground cumin, ground ginger and ground turmeric

1 tablespoon plain flour (all-purpose flour)

1½ cups (375ml) beef stock

400g (12½oz) can chickpeas (garbanzo beans), drained, rinsed

6 fresh dates (120g), pitted, chopped coarsely

1 tablespoon honey

2 tablespoons chopped fresh coriander (cilantro)

1 To make lamb filling, finely chop onion, carrot and garlic. Cut lamb into 3cm (1¼in) pieces. Heat oil in a large heavy-based saucepan; cook onion, carrot and garlic, stirring until onion softens. Add spices; cook, stirring, until fragrant. Add lamb; cook, stirring, until browned all over. Add flour; cook, stirring, until mixture thickens. Add stock and chickpeas; bring to the boil. Reduce heat; simmer, covered, for 30 minutes. Stir in dates, honey and coriander; simmer, uncovered, for 10 minutes or until sauce is thickened and lamb tender. Season to taste. Cool. (Makes 4 cups.)

2 Lightly grease and preheat a 4-hole (¾-cup/180ml) pie maker.

3 Using pastry cutter provided, cut six large rounds (15.5cm/6¼in) from shortcrust pastry and six small rounds (12cm/4¾in) from puff pastry. Line prepared holes with shortcrust pastry rounds, pressing into base and side. Refrigerate remaining pastry rounds until required.

4 Spoon ⅔ cup lamb filling into each pie case. Top with puff pastry rounds; press edges firmly to seal. Brush pastry with egg and sprinkle with cumin seeds. Close lid; cook for 8 minutes or until pastry is golden. Remove pies; transfer to a wire rack. Repeat with remaining pastry rounds, lamb filling, egg wash and cumin seeds to make 6 pies in total.

5 Serve pies with combined yoghurt and harissa.

tips To make these in a smaller pie maker, see page 7 for information on how much filling they hold, then adjust accordingly. Lamb filling and the pies will keep frozen for up to 3 months. Thaw in fridge overnight. Reheat pies in pie maker for 12 minutes.

CANNED FILLINGS

Ready-cooked ingredients straight from the can make some of the fastest savoury pies ever. Use one of our suggestions here, or scan the supermarket shelves to create your own family favourites.

1 Baked beans If you think beans on toast are the bee's knees you'll love them in a pie. Try classic style, smoked or spiced beans with cheddar or barbecued chicken. Go luxe with a half and half combo of beans with mash.

2 Tuna Pick a tuna flavour from the myriad available – try chilli, lemon and smoked tuna. Fancy a cheat's tuna mornay pie? Combine tuna with some onion-flavoured spreadable cream cheese. Or mix a can of tuna with pasta sauce.

3 Spaghetti It's not just kids who love this childhood convenience food but adults, too. Try with a halved ball of bocconcini pushed into the spaghetti. For a meatball pie, form the filling from a sausage into four 'meatballs'; cook in the pie maker first, then combine with the spaghetti.

4 Corn kernels For Mexican-inspired flavours, swap pastry for tortillas cut to size. Mix corn kernels with tomato salsa and a pinch of smoked paprika.

LAMB KORMA PIES

PREP + COOK TIME 50 MINUTES (+ COOLING) MAKES 6

ingredients

6 sheets frozen shortcrust pastry, thawed

2 sheets frozen puff pastry, thawed

1 egg, beaten lightly

mango chutney and raita, to serve

LAMB KORMA FILLING

20g (¾oz) butter

2 tablespoons olive oil

500g (1lb) lamb loin fillets, cut into 2cm (¾in) pieces

1 medium onion (150g), sliced thinly

1 clove garlic, crushed

1 tablespoon finely grated ginger

¼ cup (20g) roasted flaked almonds

⅓ cup (100g) korma paste

⅓ cup (80ml) chicken stock

½ cup (140g) greek yoghurt

1 cup (120g) frozen peas

1 medium boiled potato (200g), cut into 2cm (¾in) pieces

1 tablespoon lemon juice

⅓ cup firmly packed fresh coriander (cilantro) leaves, torn

1 To make lamb korma filling, heat half the butter with half the oil in a large saucepan; cook lamb, in batches, until browned. Remove from pan. Heat remaining butter and oil in same pan over low heat; cook onion, garlic and ginger, stirring, until onion softens. Add nuts and paste, cook, stirring, until fragrant. Return lamb to pan with stock and yoghurt; simmer over medium heat, stirring frequently, for 20 minutes or until sauce thickens. Stir in peas, potato, juice and coriander. Season to taste. Cool. (Makes 4 cups.)

2 Lightly grease and preheat a 4-hole (¾-cup/180ml) pie maker.

3 Using pastry cutter provided, cut six large rounds (15.5cm/6¼in) from shortcrust pastry and six small rounds (12cm/4¾in) from puff pastry. Line prepared holes with shortcrust pastry rounds, pressing into base and side. Refrigerate remaining pastry rounds until required.

4 Spoon ⅔ cup lamb korma filling into each pie case. Top with puff pastry rounds; press edges firmly to seal. Brush pastry with egg. Close lid; cook for 8 minutes or until pastry is golden. Remove; transfer to a wire rack. Repeat with remaining pastry rounds, lamb filling and egg wash to make 6 pies in total.

5 Serve pies with mango chutney and raita.

tips To make these in a smaller pie maker, see page 7 for information on how much filling they hold, then adjust accordingly. Pies and lamb korma filling will keep for up to 3 months in airtight containers in the freezer. Thaw in fridge overnight. Reheat the pies in pie maker for 12 minutes.

SHEPHERD'S PIES

**PREP + COOK TIME 1 HOUR 15 MINUTES (+ COOLING)
MAKES 12**

ingredients

3 cups (750g) mashed potato
60g (2oz) butter, melted
12 sheets frozen shortcrust pastry, thawed
cooking oil spray

LAMB FILLING
1 medium onion (150g)
1 large carrot (170g)
1 stalk celery (150g)
1 tablespoon olive oil
2 cloves garlic, crushed
2 portobello mushrooms (100g), chopped coarsely
500g (1lb) minced (ground) lamb
2 teaspoons mixed dried herbs
400g (12½oz) can diced tomatoes
½ cup (125ml) beef stock
⅓ cup (95g) tomato paste
¼ cup (70g) tomato sauce (ketchup)
2 tablespoons worcestershire sauce
2 bay leaves

1 To make lamb filling, finely chop onion, carrot and celery. Heat oil in a large frying pan over medium heat; cook onion, carrot, celery, garlic and mushrooms stirring, until vegetables soften. Add lamb and herbs; cook, stirring with a wooden spoon to break up lumps, for 5 minutes or until browned. Stir in tomatoes, stock, paste, sauces and bay leaves. Bring to the boil. Reduce heat; simmer for 15 minutes or until sauce thickens slightly. Season. Cool. (Makes 4½ cups.)

2 Combine mashed potato and butter in a medium bowl. Season.

3 Lightly grease and preheat a 4-hole (¾-cup/180ml) pie maker.

4 Using pastry cutter provided, cut twelve large rounds (15.5cm/6¼in) from shortcrust pastry. Line prepared holes with shortcrust pastry rounds, pressing into base and side. Refrigerate remaining pastry rounds until required.

5 Spoon a heaped ⅓ cup lamb filling into each pie case. Place ¼ cup of mashed potato on top of each pie; spread potato flush to pastry edge so there are no gaps for the filling to ooze through. Spray with oil. Close lid; cook for 8 minutes or until mash is golden. Remove pies; transfer to a wire rack. Wipe holes clean with paper towel.

6 Repeat with remaining pastry rounds, lamb filling and mash, spraying tops with oil, to make 12 pies in total; wipe holes clean with paper towel as needed between batches.

tips To make these in a smaller pie maker, see page 7 for information on how much filling they hold, then adjust accordingly. Pies and lamb filling will keep frozen for up to 3 months. Thaw in fridge overnight. These pies are best reheated in an oven or microwave.

PORK, SAGE & APPLE PIES

PREP + COOK TIME 35 MINUTES (+ COOLING) MAKES 4

ingredients

400g (12½oz) pork & fennel sausages

40g (1½oz) butter

2 small granny smith apples (260g), peeled, cored, cut into 1cm (½in) pieces

½ cup (120g) sour cream

2 tablespoons finely chopped fresh sage leaves

¼ teaspoon ground nutmeg

4 sheets frozen shortcrust pastry, thawed

2 sheets frozen puff pastry, thawed

1 egg, beaten lightly

small fresh sage leaves, extra

1 cup (300g) apple sauce

1 Slit sausages at the top with a sharp knife; squeeze out sausage meat from casings.

2 Melt butter in a large saucepan. Cook apples, stirring, for 3 minutes or until softened. Add sausage meat; cook, stirring with a wooden spoon to break up lumps, for 5 minutes or until browned. Stir in sour cream, sage and nutmeg. Season. Cool.

3 Lightly grease and preheat a 4-hole (¾-cup/180ml) pie maker.

4 Using pastry cutter provided, cut four large rounds (15.5cm/6¼in) from shortcrust pastry and four small rounds (12cm/4¾in) from puff pastry. Line prepared holes with shortcrust pastry rounds, pressing into base and side. Refrigerate remaining pastry rounds until required.

5 Spoon ⅔ cup sausage mixture into each pastry case. Top with puff pastry rounds; press edges firmly to seal. Brush pastry with egg and decorate with extra sage leaves; spray with oil. Close and cook for 8 minutes or until pastry is golden.

6 Serve pies straightaway with apple sauce.

tip To make these in a smaller pie maker, see page 7 for information on how much filling they hold, then adjust accordingly.

BUTTER CHICKEN ROTI PIES

PREP + COOK TIME 55 MINUTES (+ COOLING & REFRIGERATION) MAKES 4

ingredients

600g (1¼lb) chicken thigh fillets, fat trimmed, cut into quarters
½ cup (135g) butter chicken curry paste
⅔ cup (190g) greek yoghurt
2 teaspoons garam masala
1 clove garlic, crushed
2 teaspoons olive oil
¾ cup (210g) tomato puree
¼ cup (60ml) pouring cream
¼ cup chopped fresh coriander (cilantro) leaves
12 roti pieces (375g) (see tips)
2 tablespoons flaked almonds

1 Combine chicken, curry paste, yoghurt, garam masala and garlic in a large bowl. Cover and refrigerate for 15 minutes.

2 Heat oil in a medium saucepan. Add chicken mixture; cook, stirring, for 5 minutes or until browned. Stir in tomato puree; bring to the boil. Reduce heat; cook, covered, for 20 minutes or until chicken is cooked through and sauce is thickened. Stir in cream and coriander; simmer for a further 5 minutes. Season to taste. Cool.

3 Lightly grease and preheat a 4-hole (¾-cup/180ml) pie maker.

4 Line prepared holes with two roti squares, overlapping slightly; trim hard edges with scissors. Spoon ⅔ cup butter chicken into each roti case. Top with roti squares; press edges firmly to seal. Sprinkle with flaked almonds. Close lid; cook for 8 minutes or until roti is golden.

tips Before using the roti, flatten the bread with a rolling pin. You can use garlic naan instead if you prefer. To make these in a smaller pie maker, see page 7 for information on how much filling they hold, then adjust accordingly. Butter chicken will keep frozen for up to 3 months. Thaw in the fridge overnight before using.

FISH MORNAY & POTATO PIES

PREP + COOK TIME 35 MINUTES (+ COOLING) MAKES 4

ingredients

400g (12½oz) sebago potatoes

200g (6½oz) boneless, skinless, firm white fish fillets (such as ling)

200g (6½oz) boneless, skinless, salmon fillets

20g (¾oz) butter

1½ tablespoons plain flour (all-purpose flour)

1 cup (250ml) milk

½ cup (60g) grated cheddar

1 tablespoon chopped fresh dill

4 sheets frozen shortcrust pastry, thawed

⅓ cup (25g) panko (japanese) breadcrumbs

40g (1½oz) butter, extra, chopped

potato wedges and lemon wedges, to serve

1 Peel and cut potato into 5mm (¼in) thick slices. Boil, steam or microwave potato until tender; rinse under cold water and drain well on paper towel. Cut fish fillets into 3cm (1¼in) pieces.

2 Melt butter in a medium saucepan over medium heat. Add flour; cook, stirring, for 1 minute. Remove from heat and gradually stir in milk. Return to heat; simmer, whisking, for 3 minutes or until thickened. Whisk in half the cheese. Add fish; cook, covered, stirring halfway through, for 7 minutes or until just cooked. Stir in half the dill; season to taste. Cool.

3 Lightly grease and preheat a 4-hole (¾-cup/180ml) pie maker.

4 Using pastry cutter provided, cut four large rounds (15.5cm/6¼in) from shortcrust pastry. Line prepared holes with pastry rounds, pressing into base and side.

5 Spoon ½ cup fish mixture into each pie case; top with remaining cheese. Arrange potato slices on top, overlapping slightly. Sprinkle with combined breadcrumbs and dill; dot with butter. Close lid; cook pies for 7 minutes or until breadcrumbs are golden.

6 Serve pies with potato wedges and lemon, and any leftover mornay from the filling.

tip To make these in a smaller pie maker, see page 7 for information on how much filling they hold, then adjust accordingly.

VEGETARIAN NACHOS PIE

PREP + COOK TIME 20 MINUTES
SERVES 4

We used a family-size pie maker for this recipe.

ingredients

1 sheet frozen puff pastry, thawed

1 sheet frozen shortcrust pastry, thawed

420g (13½oz) can salsa chilli beans

½ cup (120g) sour cream

⅔ cup (160g) pickled sliced jalapeños

½ cup (120g) grated cheddar

80g (2½oz) corn chips, crushed

1 egg, beaten lightly

extra corn chips and lime wedges, to serve

GUACAMOLE

1 large avocado (320g), chopped

1 small clove garlic, crushed

1 tablespoon lime juice

1 To make guacamole, mash avocado in a bowl; stir in garlic and lime juice. Season to taste.

2 Lightly grease and preheat a family size (2½-cup/625ml) pie maker. Cut a 12cm x 40cm (4¾in x 16in) piece of baking paper; line pie maker with baking paper.

3 Using pastry cutter provided, cut one small round (23cm/9¼in) from puff pastry; refrigerate until needed. Line prepared pie maker with shortcrust pastry; press into base and side, trim excess.

4 Fill pie case with chilli beans; spoon ¼ cup sour cream on the beans, then using the back of the spoon, spread it to the edge. Top with half the jalapeños, the cheese and crushed corn chips; press down to flatten. Top with puff pastry round; press edges to seal. Brush pastry with egg. Close lid; cook pie for 12 minutes or until pastry is golden. Using baking paper for support, transfer pie to a serving plate.

5 Serve pie topped with remaining sour cream, the guacamole, remaining jalapeños, extra corn chips and lime wedges.

tip You can swap the puff pastry top for crushed corn chips if you like.

pie time

PULLED JACKFRUIT PIES WITH ASIAN SLAW

PREP + COOK TIME 45 MINUTES
MAKES 4

ingredients

1½ cups (100g) store-bought coleslaw mix

1 tablespoon thinly sliced green onion (scallion)

1 teaspoon thinly sliced red chilli (optional)

1 tablespoon fresh coriander (cilantro) leaves

1½ tablespoons vegan mayonnaise, plus extra to serve (optional)

1 sheet frozen shortcrust pastry, thawed

1 sheet frozen puff pastry, thawed

cooking oil spray

FILLING

565g (1¼lb) can young green jackfruit in brine (see tips)

½ cup (130g) hoisin sauce

2 tablespoons soy sauce

1 tablespoon rice wine vinegar

¼ teaspoon chinese five spice

1 To make filling, drain and rinse jackfruit. Cut into 1cm (½in) slices through the core. Combine hoisin, ¼ cup (60ml) water, soy sauce, vinegar and five spice in saucepan over medium heat. Season with pepper. Add jackfruit; bring to a simmer. Cook for 20 minutes, stirring and breaking jackfruit up with the back of a spoon until the sauce has thickened and the mixture resembles pulled pork. Season. Cool. (Makes 1⅓ cups.)

2 Combine coleslaw mix, green onion, chilli, coriander and mayonnaise in a small bowl.

3 Lightly grease and preheat a 4-hole (⅓-cup/80ml) pie maker.

4 Using pastry cutter provided, cut four large rounds (11cm/4½in) from shortcrust pastry and four small rounds (9.5cm/4in) from puff pastry. Line prepared holes with shortcrust pastry rounds, pressing into base and side.

5 Divide filling among pie cases. Top with puff pastry rounds; press edges firmly to seal. Spray pastry with oil. Close lid; cook for 5 minutes or until pastry is golden.

6 Serve pies topped with asian slaw and extra mayonnaise.

tips Canned jackfruit can be found at Asian supermarkets. Make sure you buy jackfruit in brine or water, not in syrup.

SWEET AS PIE

sweet as pie

EASY APPLE PIES

**PREP + COOK TIME 20 MINUTES
MAKES 4**

ingredients

385g (12oz) can apple pie slices
2 tablespoons caster sugar (superfine sugar)
1 teaspoon finely grated lemon rind
¼ teaspoon ground cinnamon
1 sheet frozen shortcrust pastry, thawed
1 sheet frozen puff pastry, thawed
1 egg, beaten lightly
1 small pink lady apple (100g) (see tips)
2 teaspoons cinnamon sugar

1 Drain canned apple slices over a small bowl; reserve 1½ tablespoons of juice, then discard remainder. Combine apple, reserved juice, caster sugar, rind and cinnamon in a medium bowl. (Makes 1¾ cups.)

2 Lightly grease and preheat a 4-hole (⅓-cup/80ml) pie maker.

3 Using pastry cutter provided, cut four large rounds (11cm/4½in) from the shortcrust pastry and four small rounds (9.5cm/4in) from the puff pastry. Line prepared holes with shortcrust pastry rounds, pressing into base and side.

4 Spoon ⅓ cup apple mixture into pie cases. Top with puff pastry rounds; press edges firmly to seal. Brush tops with egg. Decorate each pie with a fresh apple slice. Close lid; cook for 5 minutes or until golden brown.

5 Serve pies warm, sprinkled with cinnamon sugar.

tips Use a mandoline or V-slicer to cut the unpeeled apple into thin slices; slice at the last moment to avoid apple discolouring. These apple pies are best served on the day they are made, but will keep stored in an airtight container, in the fridge for up to 3 days.

ANY BERRY PIES

PREP + COOK TIME 15 MINUTES
MAKES 6

ingredients

1 cup (220g) drained canned apple pie slices, cut into 2cm (¾in) pieces
1 cup (150g) frozen berries, thawed, patted dry with paper towel (see tips)
½ cup (150g) blueberry jam
2 tablespoons caster sugar (superfine sugar)
2 teaspoons cornflour (cornstarch)
20g (¾oz) butter, chopped finely
½ teaspoon ground cinnamon
2 sheets frozen shortcrust pastry, thawed
2 sheets frozen puff pastry, thawed
1 egg, beaten lightly

1 Combine canned apple slices, berries, jam, sugar, cornflour, butter and cinnamon in a medium bowl. (Makes 2 cups.)

2 Lightly grease and preheat a 4-hole (⅓-cup/80ml) pie maker.

3 Using pastry cutter provided, cut six large rounds (11cm/4½in) from shortcrust pastry and six small rounds (9.5cm/4in) from puff pastry. Line prepared holes with shortcrust pastry rounds, pressing into base and side.

4 Spoon ⅓ cup berry mixture into pie cases. Top with puff pastry rounds; press edges firmly to seal. Using a straw, cut a small hole in the centre of each pie. Brush tops with egg. Close lid; cook for 5 minutes or until golden brown. Remove pies; transfer to a wire rack. Repeat with remaining pastry, berry mixture and egg wash to make 6 pies in total.

5 Serve pies straightaway.

tips We used blueberries, however you can use whatever type of berry you like. These pies are best served on the day they are made, but will keep stored in an airtight container, in the fridge for up to 3 days.

STRAWBERRY RHUBARB CRUMBLE PIES

PREP + COOK TIME 25 MINUTES (+ COOLING) MAKES 10

ingredients

240g (8oz) shortbread biscuits

3 sheets frozen shortcrust pastry, thawed

vanilla ice-cream, to serve

RHUBARB FILLING

½ cup (110g) caster sugar (superfine sugar)

⅓ cup (80ml) orange juice

500g (1lb) rhubarb, trimmed, cut into 5cm (2in) lengths

2 teaspoons finely grated orange rind

250g (8oz) strawberries, halved

2 teaspoons cornflour (cornstarch)

1 To make rhubarb filling, combine sugar and orange juice in a medium saucepan; stir over low heat until sugar dissolves. Bring to the boil. Reduce heat; add rhubarb and rind. Simmer, covered, for 5 minutes or until rhubarb is tender. Remove from heat; stir in strawberries and cornflour. Cool. See tip. (Makes 3 cups.)

2 Place shortbread in a zip-lock bag and, using a rolling pin, crush until fine crumbs form.

3 Lightly grease and preheat a 4-hole (⅓-cup/80ml) pie maker.

4 Using pastry cutter provided, cut ten large rounds (11cm/4½in) from shortcrust pastry. Line prepared holes with pastry rounds, pressing into base and side. Refrigerate remaining rounds until required.

5 Spoon ¼ cup rhubarb filling into pie cases. Sprinkle 2 tablespoons shortbread crumbs on each pie to cover filling. Close lid; cook for 7 minutes or until shortbread is golden brown. Remove pies; transfer to a wire rack. Repeat with remaining pastry rounds, rhubarb filling and shortbread crumbs to make 10 pies in total.

6 Serve pies warm with ice-cream.

tips If you want to make fewer than 10 pies, set aside enough filling for the number you wish to cook; freeze the remaining filling for up to 3 months. Thaw overnight in fridge before using. Crumbles will keep stored in the fridge for up to 3 days.

CHERRY LATTICE PIES

PREP + COOK TIME 25 MINUTES (+ CHILLING) MAKES 4

ingredients

2 sheets frozen shortcrust pastry, thawed
415g (13oz) canned pitted black cherries in syrup
⅓ cup (110g) cherry jam
2 tablespoons caster sugar (superfine sugar)
1 tablespoon cornflour (cornstarch)
1 teaspoon vanilla extract
1 egg, beaten lightly

1 Line an oven tray with baking paper. Place a sheet of shortcrust pastry on a floured work surface, cut into 1cm (½in) wide strips. Weave pastry strips into a lattice pattern; place on tray. Freeze for 5 minutes.

2 Meanwhile, drain cherries through a fine sieve, pressing down with the back of a spoon to extract as much syrup as possible; discard syrup. Combine cherries, jam, sugar, cornflour and vanilla in a medium bowl. (Makes 1⅓ cups.)

3 Lightly grease a 4-hole (⅓-cup/80ml) pie maker.

4 Using pastry cutter provided, cut four large rounds (11cm/4½in) from the remaining sheet of shortcrust pastry and four small rounds (9.5cm/4in) from the lattice sheet. With pie maker turned off, line prepared holes with large shortcrust pastry rounds, pressing into base and side.

5 Spoon ⅓ cup cherry mixture into pie cases. Top with shortcrust lattice rounds; press edges firmly to seal. Brush lattice with egg. Turn pie maker on. Close lid; cook for 8 minutes or until golden. Remove pies; transfer to a wire rack to cool slightly.

tip The pies are best served on the day they are made, but will keep refrigerated for up to 3 days.

RASPBERRY & FRANGIPANE TARTS

PREP + COOK TIME 35 MINUTES (+ COOLING) MAKES 6

ingredients

2 sheets frozen shortcrust pastry, thawed

75g (2½oz) raspberries (see tips)

¼ cup (80g) raspberry jam

FRANGIPANE

100g (3oz) butter, softened

½ cup (110g) caster sugar (superfine sugar)

1 teaspoon vanilla extract

2 eggs

¾ cup (90g) almond meal

2 tablespoons plain flour (all-purpose flour)

1 To make frangipane, beat butter, sugar and vanilla in a small bowl with an electric mixer until light and fluffy. Beat in eggs, one at a time. Fold in almond meal and flour. (Makes 1½ cups.)

2 Lightly grease and preheat a 4-hole (⅓-cup/80ml) pie maker.

3 Using pastry cutter provided, cut six large rounds (11cm/4½in) from shortcrust pastry. Line prepared holes with pastry rounds, pressing into base and side. Refrigerate remaining rounds until required.

4 Spoon ¼ cup frangipane mixture into tart cases; smooth surface, arrange raspberries on top. Close lid; cook for 10 minutes or until a skewer inserted into the centre comes out clean. Remove tarts; transfer to a wire rack to cool. Repeat with remaining pastry rounds, frangipane and raspberries to make 6 tarts in total. Cool.

5 Heat jam in a small heatproof bowl in the microwave on HIGH (100%) for 20 seconds or until melted. Brush cooled tarts with jam, to glaze.

tips You can also use blackberries or fresh figs instead of raspberries, if you like. Frangipane tarts are best served on the day they are made, but will keep in an airtight container, in the fridge for up to 3 days.

APRICOT DANISHES

**PREP + COOK TIME 20 MINUTES (+ STANDING)
MAKES 4**

ingredients

½ cup (125g) drained canned apricot halves in syrup (see tips)
1 sheet frozen puff pastry, thawed
2 tablespoons cream cheese
1½ tablespoons apricot jam
1 egg, beaten lightly

1 Lightly grease and preheat a 4-hole (⅓-cup/80ml) pie maker. Cut four 5cm x 15cm (2in x 6in) strips of baking paper.

2 Drain apricots on paper towel to absorb excess syrup.

3 Cut four 9cm (3¾in) squares from the puff pastry. Place baking paper strips on a work surface; top with puff pastry squares in the centre.

Place 2 teaspoons of cream cheese in the centre of each pastry square, top with 1 teaspoon of jam and 2 apricot halves (on top of each other); press down. Fold opposite corners of pastry over apricots to partially cover; brush pastry with egg.

4 Using baking paper strips for support, lift pastries into prepared holes. Close lid; cook for 10 minutes or until golden brown. Using paper strips, lift pastries from holes and transfer to a wire rack. Brush warm pastries with remaining jam; cool.

tips You can also used canned peaches or plums instead of apricots, if you like. Pastries are best eaten on the day they are made.

FRUIT MINCE PIES

PREP + COOK TIME 25 MINUTES (+ COOLING)
MAKES 8

ingredients

820g (1¾lb) jar fruit mince

1 cup (160g) finely chopped dried apricots

2 tablespoons brandy

2 sheets frozen shortcrust pastry, thawed

2 sheets frozen puff pastry, thawed

1 egg, beaten lightly

1 tablespoon icing sugar (confectioners' sugar)

1 Combine fruit mince, apricots and brandy in a medium bowl.

2 Lightly grease and preheat a 4-hole (⅓-cup/80ml) pie maker.

3 Using pastry cutter provided, cut eight large rounds (11cm/4½in) from shortcrust pastry and eight small rounds (9.5cm/4in) from puff pastry. Using a 4cm (1½in) star cutter, cut out four stars from four puff pastry rounds; reserve. Line prepared holes with shortcrust pastry rounds, pressing into base and side.

4 Spoon ⅓ cup fruit mince into pie cases. Top with puff pastry rounds; press edges firmly to seal. Brush tops with egg. Close lid; cook for 5 minutes or until golden brown. Remove pies; transfer to a wire rack. Repeat with remaining pastry rounds, filling and egg.

5 Spray holes with oil; place a pastry star into each hole. Close lid; cook for 3 minutes. Turn stars over; cook for further 3 minutes or until golden and puffed. Remove stars; transfer to a wire rack to cool.

6 Place pastry stars on plain pies. Serve all pies dusted with sifted icing sugar.

tip Mince pies will keep stored in an airtight container, in the refrigerator for up to 5 days.

CHEAT'S LEMON MERINGUE PIES

PREP + COOK TIME 15 MINUTES (+ COOLING)
MAKES 4

ingredients

1 sheet frozen shortcrust pastry, thawed
⅔ cup (200g) bought lemon curd
40g (1½oz) white mini marshmallows (see tip)

1 Lightly grease and preheat a 4-hole (⅓-cup/80ml) pie maker.

2 Using pastry cutter provided, cut four large rounds (11cm/4½in) from shortcrust pastry. Line prepared holes with shortcrust pastry rounds, pressing into base and side. Close lid; cook for 5 minutes or until pastry is golden. Remove pie cases from holes; cool on a wire rack.

3 Spoon 2 tablespoons lemon curd into each cooled pie cases (be careful not to over fill, there should be a 2mm (1/12in) gap below pie rim); smooth the surface. Arrange mini marshmallows in a circular pattern on top of curd.

4 Return assembled pies to pie maker. Close lid; cook for 1 minute or until marshmallows are light golden and just starting to melt (be careful not to overheat or the marshmallows will stick to the lid). Serve pies straightaway.

tip If you can't find mini marshmallows, you could cut regular-sized marshmallows into 1cm (½in) pieces instead.

CLASSIC CUSTARD TARTS

PREP + COOK TIME 30 MINUTES (+ COOLING) MAKES 8

ingredients

2 sheets frozen shortcrust pastry, thawed

1 cup (250ml) pouring cream

⅓ cup (75g) caster sugar (superfine sugar)

3 eggs

2 teaspoons vanilla extract

¼ teaspoon ground nutmeg, plus extra to serve

1 Lightly grease and preheat a 4-hole (⅓-cup/80ml) pie maker.

2 Using pastry cutter provided, cut eight large rounds (11cm/4½in) from shortcrust pastry. Line prepared holes with shortcrust pastry rounds, pressing into base and side. Close lid; cook for 2 minutes or until pastry is light golden. Remove tart cases from holes; transfer to a wire rack to cool. Repeat with remaining pastry rounds.

3 Whisk cream, caster sugar, eggs, vanilla and nutmeg in a large jug. (Makes 2½ cups.)

4 Place cooled tart cases on a tray; pour a scant ¼ cup custard filling into each (be careful not to over fill, there should be a 2mm (1/12in) gap below tart rim).

5 Place custard tarts back in pie maker holes. Close lid; cook for 10 minutes or until custard is set. Remove tarts; transfer to a wire rack to cool. Repeat with remaining custard tarts.

6 Serve custard tarts sprinkled with extra nutmeg.

tip Custard tarts are best served on the day they are made, but will keep stored in the refrigerator for up to 3 days.

COCONUT & PASSIONFRUIT IMPOSSIBLE PIES

PREP + COOK TIME 35 MINUTES
MAKES 11

ingredients

2 x 170g (5½oz) cans passionfruit pulp in syrup (see tips)
¼ cup (35g) plain flour (all-purpose flour)
½ cup (110g) caster sugar (superfine sugar)
½ cup (40g) desiccated coconut
2 eggs, beaten lightly
1 teaspoon vanilla extract
60g (2oz) butter, melted
⅔ cups (160ml) milk
1 tablespoon icing sugar (confectioners' sugar)
whipped cream and passionfruit pulp (see tips), to serve

1 Lightly grease and preheat a 4-hole (⅓-cup/80ml) pie maker.

2 Drain canned passionfruit pulp through a sieve into a small jug or bowl. You will need ¼ cup passionfruit seeds.

3 Sift flour into medium bowl; stir in caster sugar, coconut, eggs, vanilla, melted butter, milk and ¼ cup of passionfruit seeds.

4 Pour a scant ¼ cup of mixture into prepared holes (be careful not to over fill, there should be a 3mm (⅛in) gap from top). Close lid; cook for 10 minutes or until set. Gently remove pies; transfer to a baking-paper-covered wire rack to cool. Repeat with remaining mixture to make 11 pies in total.

5 Serve dusted with sifted icing sugar and topped with cream and passionfruit pulp.

tips You can use fresh passionfruit instead of canned for this recipe; you will need 3 passionfruit for the filling and 2 to serve. The base of these pies will develop a layer of custard during cooking.

JAR FILLINGS

A good pie is a sum of its parts – good pastry and tasty filling. While you can plan your filling in advance your pantry can also be the source for many instant ones, so that anytime can become pie time!

1 **Nutella** This chocolate hazelnut spread can be put to use all on its own for a ridiculously rich pie or tart, or try it mixed with your favourite crumbled biscuit, nuts, cake leftovers or with frozen raspberries.

2 **Jams** Pick your favourite flavour. For a peach melba inspired pie, spread a little jam in the base of your pie case and top with drained canned peaches.

3 **Dulce de Leche** This rich South American caramel sauce is definitely for the sweet tooth. Mix with drained canned pie apples or pears. Or beat an egg with ½ cup caramel to use as a filling. For a salted caramel flavour, add a pinch of salt flakes. Or mix the caramel with salted peanuts.

4 **Lemon curd** Try this tangy spread all on its own or layer in a pie case with either a spoonful of ricotta or sour cream.

EASY COOKIES & CREAM PIES

PREP + COOK TIME 10 MINUTES
MAKES 4

ingredients

8 Oreo biscuits (80g)
1 sheet frozen shortcrust pastry, thawed
1 sheet frozen puff pastry, thawed
12 white marshmallows (70g)
2 tablespoons thick (double) cream
2 tablespoons chocolate sauce (see tip)

1 Place Oreos in a zip-top bag; using a rolling pin, crush until fine crumbs form.

2 Lightly grease and preheat a 4-hole (⅓-cup/80ml) pie maker.

3 Using pastry cutter provided, cut four large rounds (11cm/4½in) from shortcrust pastry and four small rounds (9.5cm/4in) from puff pastry. Line prepared holes with shortcrust pastry rounds, pressing into base and side.

4 Divide Oreo crumbs and marshmallows among pie cases. Top with puff pastry rounds; press edges firmly to seal. Close lid; cook for 5 minutes or until golden. Remove pies; transfer to a wire rack.

5 Serve pies straightaway topped with cream and chocolate sauce.

tip For the chocolate sauce, you can use chocolate dessert sauce or chocolate ice-cream topping.

PEACHES & CREAM PIES

PREP + COOK TIME 20 MINUTES
MAKES 6

ingredients

2 sheets frozen shortcrust pastry, thawed
2 sheets frozen puff pastry, thawed
200g (6½oz) cream cheese, softened
½ cup (160g) apricot jam
410g (13oz) can peach slices in juice, drained
1 egg, beaten lightly
2 tablespoons apricot jam, extra
vanilla ice-cream, to serve

1 Lightly grease and preheat a 4-hole (⅓-cup/80ml) pie maker.

2 Using pastry cutter provided, cut six large rounds (11cm/4½in) from shortcrust pastry and six small rounds (9.5cm/4in) from puff pastry. Line prepared holes with shortcrust pastry rounds, pressing into base and side.

3 Spread 1 tablespoon cream cheese and 2 teaspoons jam on pastry bases. Arrange 4 peach slices on top, followed by 1 teaspoon cream cheese. Top with puff pastry rounds; press edges to seal. Brush tops with egg.

4 Close lid; cook pies for 5 minutes or until golden. Remove pies; transfer to a wire rack. Repeat with remaining pastry rounds, filling and egg to make 6 pies in total.

5 Microwave extra jam in a small heatproof bowl on HIGH (100%) for 20 seconds or until melted. Serve pies topped with a scoop of ice-cream, drizzled with warm jam.

sweet as pie

KEY LIME PIES

**PREP + COOK TIME 50 MINUTES (+ COOLING)
MAKES 14**

ingredients

4 sheets frozen shortcrust pastry, thawed
4 egg yolks
395g (12½oz) can sweetened condensed milk
1 tablespoon finely grated lime rind
½ cup (125ml) lime juice
½ cup (125ml) thickened cream (heavy cream)
thinly sliced lime and lime rind, and mint leaves, to serve

1 Lightly grease and preheat a 4-hole (⅓-cup/80ml) pie maker.

2 Using pastry cutter provided, cut 14 large rounds (11cm/4½in) from shortcrust pastry. Line prepared holes with shortcrust pastry rounds, pressing into base and side. Close lid; cook for 2 minutes or until pastry is light golden. Remove pastry cases from holes; cool on a wire rack. Repeat with remaining pastry rounds.

3 Beat egg yolks in a small bowl with an electric mixer on high speed for 4 minutes or until light and fluffy. Beat in condensed milk, rind and juice on low speed.

4 Place cooled pie cases on a tray; pour lime filling evenly into each (be careful not to over fill, there should be a 3mm (⅛in) gap below the rim).

5 Place filled pie cases back in pie maker holes. Close lid; cook for 8 minutes or until filling is set. Remove pies; transfer to a wire rack to cool. Repeat with remaining filled pie cases.

6 Beat cream in a small bowl with electric mixer until firm peaks form.

7 Serve pies topped with cream, lime slices and rind, and mint.

tips To pimp the pies further you can make a syrup with equal parts sugar dissolved in boiling water with the lime rind. Key lime pies will keep, stored in an airtight container, in the refrigerator for up to 5 days.

CARTWHEELS

**PREP + COOK TIME 20 MINUTES
MAKES 8**

ingredients

8 shortbread biscuits (130g)

2 sheets frozen shortcrust pastry, thawed

2 sheets frozen puff pastry, thawed

⅔ cup (220g) raspberry jam

⅓ cup (65g) milk Choc Bits

4 jumbo white marshmallows (100g), halved crossways

200g (6½oz) dark chocolate (70% cocoa), chopped coarsely

15g (½oz) freeze-dried raspberries, crushed (optional)

1 Place shortbread in a zip-lock bag; using a rolling pin, crush until fine crumbs form.

2 Lightly grease and preheat a 4-hole (⅓-cup/80ml) pie maker.

3 Using pastry cutter provided, cut eight large rounds (11cm/4½in) from shortcrust pastry and eight small rounds (9.5cm/4in) from puff pastry. Line prepared holes with shortcrust pastry rounds, pressing into base and side.

4 Divide half the shortbread crumbs among pie cases; firmly pressing into base and side with the back of a spoon. Top with half each of the jam, Choc Bits and marshmallow. Top with four puff pastry rounds; press edges to seal. Close lid; cook for 5 minutes or until golden. Remove pies; transfer to a wire rack to cool. Repeat with remaining pastry rounds, shortbread crumbs, jam, Choc Bits and marshmallow.

5 Place dark chocolate in a small heatproof bowl over a small saucepan of simmering water (make sure the water doesn't touch the base of the bowl); stir until smooth. Dip the top of each cooled pie into melted chocolate and sprinkle with crushed freeze-dried raspberries. Stand until set.

CARAMEL PECAN PIES

PREP + COOK TIME 50 MINUTES (+ COOLING)
MAKES 10

ingredients

3 sheets frozen shortcrust pastry, thawed

380g (12oz) can caramel top 'n' fill

4 egg yolks, beaten lightly

2 tablespoons brown sugar

2 teaspoons vanilla extract

½ cup (60g) finely chopped pecans

2 tablespoons thickened cream (heavy cream)

chopped roasted pecans and whipped cream, to serve

1 Lightly grease and preheat a 4-hole (⅓-cup/80ml) pie maker.

2 Using pastry cutter provided, cut ten large rounds (11cm/4½in) from shortcrust pastry. Line prepared holes with pastry rounds, pressing into base and side. Close lid; cook for 2 minutes or until pastry is light golden. Remove pie cases from holes; cool on a wire rack. Repeat with remaining pastry rounds.

3 Reserve 2 tablespoons of caramel top 'n' fill in a small bowl. Whisk remaining caramel top 'n' fill, egg yolks, brown sugar and vanilla in a medium bowl. Stir through finely chopped pecans. (Makes 1¼ cups.)

4 Place cooled pie cases on a tray; pour caramel mixture evenly among cases (be careful not to over fill, there should be a 2mm (1/12in) gap below pie rim). Place four filled pie cases back in the pie maker. Close lid; cook for 10 minutes or until set. Remove pies; transfer to a wire rack to cool. Repeat with remaining filled pie cases.

5 Meanwhile, add thickened cream to reserved caramel top 'n' fill in bowl; whisk until smooth. Spoon caramel cream over pies.

6 Serve pies topped with chopped pecans and whipped cream.

tip Undecorated pecan pies (complete to the end of step 4) will keep, stored in an airtight container, in the fridge for up to 3 days.

Chocolate Fudge Caramel Tarts

PREP + COOK TIME 25 MINUTES
MAKES 4

ingredients

1 sheet frozen shortcrust pastry, thawed
2 jersey caramels
1 teaspoon sea salt flakes, to serve

FUDGE FILLING

50g (1½oz) butter, chopped
50g (1½oz) dark (semi-sweet) chocolate, chopped coarsely
¼ cup (55g) firmly packed brown sugar
1 egg, beaten lightly
½ teaspoon vanilla extract
¼ cup (35g) plain flour (all-purpose flour)
2 teaspoons cocoa powder
¼ teaspoon fine sea salt

1 To make fudge filling, place butter and chocolate in a saucepan over low heat. Cook, stirring, for 5 minutes or until melted and smooth. Remove from heat. Stir in sugar, then egg and vanilla; mix well. Sift flour, cocoa powder and salt over chocolate mixture; stir until combined. (Makes ¾ cup.)

2 Lightly grease and preheat a 4-hole (⅓-cup/80ml) pie maker.

3 Using pastry cutter provided, cut four large rounds (11cm/4½in) from shortcrust pastry. Line prepared holes with pastry rounds, pressing into base and side.

4 Pour fudge filling evenly into tart cases. Close lid; cook for 9 minutes or until filling is risen and nearly firm to touch.

5 Meanwhile, cut jersey caramels in half horizontally; discard white filling. Place one caramel half on top of each tart. Close lid; cook for a further minute or until caramel is soft. Remove pies; transfer to a wire rack to cool slightly.

6 Serve pies sprinkled with sea salt flakes.

tip Choc fudge caramel tarts will keep, stored in an airtight container, at room temperature for up to 3 days.

sweet as pie

MISSISSIPPI MUD PIES

PREP + COOK TIME 25 MINUTES (+ COOLING) MAKES 8

ingredients
2 sheets frozen shortcrust pastry, thawed
½ cup (125ml) thickened cream (heavy cream)
200g (6½oz) chocolate mousse
white and dark chocolate curls and cocoa powder, to serve

MUD CAKE FILLING
60g (2oz) butter, chopped
½ cup (110g) caster sugar (superfine sugar)
40g (1½oz) dark (semi-sweet) chocolate, chopped coarsely
1½ tablespoons coffee-flavoured liqueur (optional)
2 teaspoons instant coffee granules
½ cup (75g) plain flour (all-purpose flour)
1 tablespoon cocoa powder
½ teaspoon bicarbonate of soda (baking soda)
pinch of salt
1 egg, beaten lightly

1 To make mud cake filling, combine butter, sugar, chocolate, ¼ cup (60ml) hot water, liqueur and coffee granules in a small saucepan; stir over low heat, without boiling, until chocolate melts. Transfer mixture to a medium bowl; cool for 15 minutes. Whisk in combined sifted flour, cocoa, bicarb soda and salt, then egg. (Makes 1½ cups.)

2 Lightly grease and preheat a 4-hole (⅓-cup/80ml) pie maker.

3 Using pastry cutter provided, cut eight large rounds (11cm/4½in) from shortcrust pastry. Line prepared holes with pastry rounds, pressing into base and side. Refrigerate remaining rounds until required.

4 Spoon 2 tablespoons mud cake filling into pie cases. Close lid; cook for 8 minutes or until risen and firm to touch. Remove pies; transfer to a wire rack to cool. Repeat with remaining pastry rounds and mud cake filling.

5 Beat cream in a small bowl with an electric mixer until firm peaks form.

6 Serve pies topped with chocolate mousse, whipped cream and chocolate curls; dust with cocoa.

tip Pies are best served on the day they are made. Undecorated mud pies (complete to the end of step 4) will keep in an airtight container, at room temperature for up to 3 days.

BLACK FOREST PIE

PREP + COOK TIME 15 MINUTES (+ COOLING) SERVES 8

We used a family-size pie maker for this recipe.

ingredients

1 sheet frozen shortcrust pastry, thawed

½ cup (125ml) thickened cream (heavy cream)

200g (6½oz) chocolate mousse

2 tablespoons cherry jam

⅓ cup (40g) fresh cherries, halved, pitted

whole fresh cherries, extra, and dark chocolate curls (see tips), to serve

1 Lightly grease a family-size (2½-cup/625ml) pie maker.

2 Line prepared pie maker with shortcrust pastry; press into base and side, then trim excess. Prick base with a fork. Turn pie maker on. Close lid; cook for 10 minutes or until pastry is golden. Remove pie case; transfer to a wire rack to cool.

3 Beat cream in a small bowl with an electric mixer until firm peaks form.

4 Spoon chocolate mousse into cooled pastry case; smooth surface. Top with whipped cream, jam and halved cherries. Decorate with whole cherries and chocolate curls.

tips If you like, use a crumbled Flake chocolate bar instead of the chocolate curls. For individual pies, using pastry cutter provided, cut four large rounds (11cm/4½in) from shortcrust pastry cook for 5 minutes then divide fillings among pie cases.

CHOC-PEANUT BUTTER BROWNIE PIES

PREP + COOK TIME 35 MINUTES
MAKES 6

ingredients

100g (3oz) butter, chopped
100g (3oz) dark (semi-sweet) chocolate, chopped coarsely
½ cup (110g) firmly packed brown sugar
2 eggs, beaten lightly
1 teaspoon vanilla extract
½ cup (75g) plain flour (all-purpose flour)
1 tablespoon cocoa powder
¼ cup (70g) smooth peanut butter, plus extra to serve
6 small scoops vanilla ice-cream
2 tablespoons coarsely chopped unsalted roasted peanuts
2 tablespoons choc fudge sauce

1 Lightly grease and preheat a 4-hole (⅓-cup/80ml) pie maker.

2 Stir butter and chocolate in a saucepan over low heat for 5 minutes or until melted and smooth. Remove from heat. Stir in sugar, then eggs and vanilla; mix well. Sift flour and cocoa powder over chocolate mixture; stir until combined.

3 Spoon 2 tablespoons brownie mixture into each prepared hole. Drop 2 teaspoons peanut butter in the centre, then cover with another 2 tablespoons brownie mixture. Close lid; cook for 12 minutes or until risen and firm to touch. Remove pies; transfer to a wire rack to cool. Repeat with remaining brownie mixture and peanut butter to make 6 pies in total.

4 Serve brownie pies topped with vanilla ice-cream, extra peanut butter, the peanuts and chocolate fudge sauce.

tip Pies will keep, stored in an airtight container, at room temperature for up to 3 days.

BANOFFEE PIES

PREP + COOK TIME 20 MINUTES (+ COOLING & REFRIGERATION) MAKES 8

ingredients

2 sheets frozen shortcrust pastry, thawed
380g (12oz) can caramel top 'n' fill
150g (4½oz) cream cheese, softened
2 tablespoons pure maple syrup
1 teaspoon vanilla extract
½ cup (125ml) thickened cream (heavy cream)
2 medium bananas (400g), sliced thinly
2 teaspoons cocoa powder
2 teaspoons icing sugar (confectioners' sugar)

1 Lightly grease and preheat a 4-hole (⅓-cup/80ml) pie maker.

2 Using pastry cutter provided, cut eight large rounds (11cm/4½in) from shortcrust pastry. Line prepared holes with shortcrust pastry rounds, pressing into base and side. Close lid; cook for 5 minutes or until pastry is golden. Remove pie cases; transfer to a wire rack to cool. Repeat with remaining pastry rounds.

3 Beat caramel top 'n' fill, cream cheese, maple syrup and vanilla in a medium bowl with an electric mixer until smooth. Place cooled cases on a lined tray. Pour caramel mixture evenly into pie cases. Refrigerate pies for 2 hours or until chilled and thickened slightly.

4 Beat cream in a small bowl with electric mixer until firm peaks form.

5 Just before serving, arrange banana slices on caramel; top with whipped cream. Dust pies with combined sifted cocoa powder and icing sugar.

tip Banoffee pies are best eaten on the day they are made. Undecorated banoffee pies (complete to the end of step 3), will keep stored in an airtight container, in the fridge for up to 3 days.

SWEET STUFF

sweet stuff

CHOCOLATE COOKIES

PREP + COOK TIME 1 HOUR 35 MINUTES (+ COOLING & REFRIGERATION) MAKES 32

ingredients

2 cups (300g) plain flour (all-purpose flour)
½ cup (50g) cocoa powder
½ teaspoon bicarbonate of soda (baking soda)
½ teaspoon salt
180g (5½oz) butter, softened
1 cup (220g) firmly packed brown sugar
¼ cup (55g) caster sugar (superfine sugar)
1½ teaspoons vanilla extract
1 egg
1 egg yolk
1 cup (190g) milk chocolate chips
100g (3oz) dark (semi-sweet) chocolate, chopped coarsely
Nutella, to serve (optional)

1 Sift flour, cocoa, bicarb soda and salt into a large bowl.

2 Beat butter and sugars in a large bowl with an electric mixer until pale and creamy. Beat in vanilla, egg and egg yolk until just combined. Fold in the sifted dry ingredients. Stir in three-quarters each of the chocolate chips and the chopped chocolate.

3 Place a 30cm x 60cm (12in x 24in) sheet of baking paper on a work surface. Place cookie mixture lengthways down the centre of the paper forming it into a 35cm (14in) long log shape; roll up to enclose in the baking paper, so that the diameter of the log is 5cm (2in). Refrigerate for 1 hour.

4 Cut cookie log into 1cm (½in) thick rounds; you should have 32 cookies. Gently press remaining chocolate chips and chopped chocolate on tops of the cookies (see tips).

5 Lightly grease and preheat a 4-hole (⅓-cup/80ml) pie maker.

6 Place cookie dough rounds in prepared holes. Close lid; cook for 10 minutes or until risen. Cookies will be soft to touch but firm up on cooling. Gently remove cookies; transfer to a wire rack to cool completely. Repeat in batches with remaining cookie rounds. Serve cookies topped with a dollop of Nutella.

tips Cookie dough freezes well. Set aside how many you wish to cook then place remaining cookie dough rounds on lined trays; cover and freeze overnight or until firm. Store frozen cookie dough rounds in zip-top bags for up to 3 months. Cook from frozen adding an extra 2 minutes to the cooking time.

sweet stuff

S'MORES

PREP + COOK TIME 8 MINUTES MAKES 4

ingredients

8 dark chocolate digestive biscuits

2 jumbo white marshmallows, halved crossways

1 Lightly grease and preheat a 4-hole (⅓-cup/80ml) pie maker. Cut eight 3cm x 15cm (1¼in x 6in) strips of baking paper. Line holes with two criss-crossed strips of baking paper.

2 Using a 5.5cm (2¼in) round cookie cutter, cut eight rounds from the biscuits, so they fit into the holes (see tip).

3 Sandwich marshmallow halves between two biscuits, chocolate sides facing inward. Place biscuit sandwiches in prepared holes. Close lid; cook for 2 minutes or until marshmallows are melted and chocolate is oozing. Using baking paper strips, carefully lift s'mores from holes onto plates. Serve straightaway.

tip If using a larger 4-hole (¾-cup/80ml) pie maker, you can skip this step.

JAM DOUGHNUTS

PREP + COOK TIME 30 MINUTES
MAKES 6

ingredients

290g (9oz) packet baked doughnut mix (see tips)
⅓ cup (80ml) vegetable oil
1 egg, beaten lightly
¼ cup (60ml) milk
⅓ cup (110g) raspberry jam
½ cup (110g) caster sugar (superfine sugar)
1 teaspoon ground cinnamon

1 Place doughnut mix into a large bowl with oil, egg, milk and 1 tablespoon water; stir until batter is smooth.

2 Lightly grease and preheat a 4-hole (⅓-cup/80ml) pie maker.

3 Spoon 2 tablespoons of batter into prepared holes. Drop heaped teaspoon of jam in the middle of each, then spoon 1 teaspoon of the batter over to cover jam. Close lid; cook for 10 minutes or until a skewer inserted in the centre comes out clean. Transfer to a wire rack. Repeat with remaining mixture and a little more jam to make 6 doughnuts in total.

4 Toss warm doughnuts in combined sugar and cinnamon.

5 Spoon remaining jam into a piping bag fitted with a small plain nozzle. Using a small sharp knife, cut a small slit in the side of each doughnut. Insert piping nozzle into cross and squeeze in filling until you feel the weight of the doughnut increase slightly. Serve warm.

tips Most doughnut packet mixes include a sachet of icing or glaze, set this aside for another use. For variety you could fill the doughnuts with thick vanilla custard or Nutella instead of jam.

FUNFETTI DOUGHNUTS

PREP
+ COOK
TIME
50 MINUTES
(+ COOLING)
MAKES
12

ingredients

2 x 290g (9oz) packets baked doughnut mix (see tip)

¾ cup (180ml) vegetable oil, plus 1 teaspoon extra

2 eggs, beaten lightly

½ cup (125ml) milk

250g (8oz) white cooking chocolate, chopped coarsely

150g (4½oz) dark (semi-sweet) chocolate, chopped coarsely

pink food colouring

assorted coloured sprinkles and shredded coconut, to decorate

1 Place doughnut mix into a large bowl with oil, egg, milk and 1 tablespoon water; stir until batter is smooth.

2 Lightly grease and preheat a 4-hole (⅓-cup/80ml) pie maker.

3 Pour ¼ cup batter into prepared holes. Close lid; cook for 10 minutes or until a skewer inserted in the centre comes out clean. Remove; transfer to a wire rack to cool. Repeat with the remaining mixture to make 12 doughnuts in total.

4 Using a small round cutter or an apple corer, cut a hole in the centre of each doughnut, to create a traditional doughnut shape. Place doughnuts on a tray in the freezer to chill while you prepare the glaze.

5 Place white chocolate in medium heatproof bowl over a medium saucepan of simmering water (make sure the water doesn't touch the bowl); stir until smooth. Stir in the extra oil. Repeat melting with dark chocolate. Divide white chocolate into two small bowls; add a few drops of pink food colouring to one and stir to combine.

6 Dip tops of cooled doughnuts into chocolates and/or drizzle and decorate with sprinkles and coconut as pictured. Stand until set.

tip Most doughnut packet mixes include a sachet of icing or glaze, set this aside for another use.

EASY-AS-PIE ICE-CREAM SANDWICHES

PREP + COOK TIME 1 HOUR (+ COOLING & FREEZING) MAKES 8

ingredients

1 litre (4 cups) salted caramel ice-cream, softened

200g (6½oz) chocolate-covered honeycomb pieces, chopped coarsely

450g (14oz) ready-to-bake choc chip cookie dough (see tips)

200g (6½oz) dark chocolate (70% cocoa), chopped coarsely

2 teaspoons vegetable oil

honeycomb pieces, crushed, to decorate

1 Grease a 23cm (9in) square cake pan; line base and sides with baking paper, extending the paper 5cm (2in) above the sides.

2 Place softened ice-cream in a large bowl. Fold in chocolate honeycomb. Spoon mixture into pan; smooth surface. Freeze for 2 hours or overnight until firm.

3 Lightly grease and preheat a 4-hole (⅓-cup/80ml) pie maker.

4 Cut cookie dough into sixteen 1cm (½in) thick slices. Place a cookie dough round in prepared holes. Close lid; cook for 10 minutes or until golden around edges. Gently remove cookies; transfer to a wire rack to cool completely. Repeat with remaining cookie dough rounds.

5 Lift ice-cream from pan onto a chopping board. Using a 6cm (2½in) round cutter, cut eight rounds from ice-cream. Reserve off-cuts for another use. Sandwich ice-cream rounds between two cookies. Place on a baking-paper-lined tray; return to freezer for 30 minutes or until firm.

6 Place chocolate and oil in a medium heatproof bowl over a medium saucepan of simmering water (make sure the water doesn't touch the base of the bowl); stir until smooth. Pour chocolate into a small wide glass (this will make it easier to dip the ice-cream sandwiches).

7 Half dip ice-cream sandwiches, one at a time, into chocolate. Gently shake off excess chocolate and sprinkle with crushed honeycomb. Place on a lined tray (or balance on egg rings, choc-dipped half facing up); freeze for 10 minutes or until chocolate is set.

tips Ready-to-bake cookie dough is a chilled product; you'll find it in the refrigerated section of most supermarkets. For variety you could use chocolate flavoured ice-cream instead of salted caramel, and M&M's or choc chips instead of honeycomb. This recipe is best made the day before serving to allow the ice-cream sandwiches time to firm.

Pikelets with Raspberries & Crème Fraîche

PREP + COOK TIME 45 MINUTES
MAKES 22

ingredients
1 cup (150g) self-raising flour
1 tablespoon caster sugar (superfine sugar)
1 egg
1¼ cups (310ml) buttermilk
25g (¾oz) butter, melted
cinnamon sugar, to serve
½ cup (120g) crème fraîche
⅓ cup (110g) raspberry jam
½ cup (70g) fresh raspberries

1 Sift flour and sugar in a medium bowl. Whisk egg, buttermilk and melted butter in a medium jug. Gradually whisk egg mixture into flour mixture until smooth.

2 Preheat and grease a 4-hole (⅓-cup/80ml) pie maker.

3 Pour 1 tablespoon of batter into prepared holes. Close lid; cook pikelets for 3 minutes or until starting to set. Gently turn with a small rubber spatula; close lid and cook for a further 3 minutes or until lightly browned. Remove pikelets; transfer to a baking-paper-lined tray. Repeat with remaining mixture to make 22 pikelets in total; grease holes as needed between batches.

4 Sprinkle pikelets with cinnamon sugar. Serve topped with crème fraîche, raspberry jam and fresh raspberries.

tip To freeze pikelets, place cooled pikelets, in a single layer, on lined trays; cover and freeze until firm. Store frozen pikelets in zip-top bags for up to 3 months. Thaw before warming in the micorwave on HIGH (100%) power for 25 seconds. Or wrap in foil in bundles of three and reheat in the pie maker for 12 minutes.

sweet stuff

CINNAMON SCROLLS

PREP + COOK TIME 40 MINUTES (+ COOLING) MAKES 12

ingredients

2 cups (300g) self-raising flour

½ teaspoon bicarbonate of soda (baking soda)

1 teaspoon salt

50g (1½oz) cold butter, chopped coarsely

¾ cup (180ml) buttermilk, approximately

60g (2oz) butter, extra, softened

¼ cup (55g) caster sugar (superfine sugar)

2 teaspoons ground cinnamon

cooking oil spray

ICING

½ cup (80g) icing sugar (confectioners' sugar)

1 tablespoon milk

1 Sift flour, bicarb soda and salt into a bowl; rub in chopped butter with your fingertips. Add enough buttermilk to mix to a soft, sticky dough. Turn dough onto a floured work surface; knead lightly until smooth. Roll out dough into a 30cm x 40cm (12in x 16in) rectangle.

2 Lightly grease and preheat a 4-hole (⅓-cup/80ml) pie maker. Cut 12 x 5.5cm (2¼in) rounds from baking paper. Line holes with baking paper rounds.

3 Spread dough with extra butter; sprinkle with combined sugar and cinnamon (leaving a 2cm (¾in) border along the top long edge). Spray border with oil spray. Roll dough tightly from the long edge nearest you; pinch seam to seal. Using a serrated knife, trim the ends. Cut roll into 12 x 3cm (1¼in) thick, slices.

4 Place scrolls, cut-side down, into prepared holes; spray with oil. Close lid; cook for 8 minutes or until risen and golden. Transfer scrolls to a wire rack to cool. Repeat in batches with remaining scrolls; wipe holes clean with paper towel as needed and reline with baking paper rounds.

5 To make icing, whisk sifted icing sugar and milk in a small bowl until smooth and runny. Dip scrolls into icing, place on a baking-paper-covered wire rack. Stand until set before serving.

variation
NUTELLA SCROLLS

Swap the butter, sugar and cinnamon with ⅔ cup (220g) Nutella and ½ cup (60g) finely chopped hazelnuts. Continue as directed in the recipe. Drizzle scrolls with icing and sprinkle with more finely chopped hazelnuts.

LAMINGTONS

PREP + COOK TIME 45 MINUTES (+ COOLING) MAKES 8

ingredients

3 eggs

⅓ cup (75g) caster sugar (superfine sugar)

¼ cup (35g) plain flour (all-purpose flour)

2 tablespoons self-raising flour

2 tablespoons cornflour (cornstarch)

1½ cups (120g) desiccated coconut

½ cup (125ml) thickened cream (heavy cream)

CHOCOLATE ICING

2 cups (320g) icing sugar (confectioners' sugar)

¼ cup (35g) cocoa powder

10g (½oz) butter, melted

½ cup (125ml) milk

1 Lightly grease and preheat a 4-hole (⅓-cup/80ml) pie maker.

2 Beat eggs in a medium bowl with an electric mixer for 10 minutes or until thick and creamy. Gradually add sugar, beating until dissolved between additions. Fold in triple-sifted flours (see tip).

3 Spoon ¼ cup mixture into prepared holes. Close lid; cook for 6 minutes or until a skewer inserted into centre comes out clean. Gently transfer cakes to a wire rack to cool. Repeat with remaining mixture.

4 To make chocolate icing, sift icing sugar and cocoa into a medium heatproof bowl; stir in butter and milk. Place bowl over a medium saucepan of simmering water; stir until icing becomes a coating consistency.

5 Place coconut in a bowl. Dip cooled cakes in icing; drain off excess. Toss in coconut. Place on a baking-paper-covered wire rack to set.

6 Beat cream in a small bowl with electric mixer until firm peaks form.

7 Just before serving, split lamingtons in half and fill with whipped cream.

tip To triple-sift flours, sift flours onto a piece of baking paper. Lift the baking paper up and repeat sifting onto another piece of baking paper for a second time. For the third sifting, hold the sifter up high as you sift over the egg mixture, seconds before you start folding the ingredients together. Doing this will assist in creating extra lightness.

sweet stuff

BAKED LEMON MANGO CHEESECAKE

PREP + COOK TIME 30 MINUTES (+ COOLING & REFRIGERATION) MAKES 8

ingredients

80g (2½oz) plain sweet biscuits
45g (1½oz) butter, melted
250g (8oz) cream cheese, softened
½ cup (110g) caster sugar (superfine sugar)
2 eggs
1 teaspoon finely grated lemon rind
1 tablespoon lemon juice
1 small mango (300g)
blueberries, lemon rind strips and mint leaves, to serve

1 Place eight ⅓ cup (80ml) paper cases on a tray (see tip).

2 Process biscuits until fine crumbs form; transfer to a small bowl. Add butter; stir through until evenly combined. Press 1 tablespoon biscuit mixture into base of each paper case; freeze for 5 minutes or until firm.

3 Meanwhile, beat cream cheese and sugar in a small bowl with an electric mixer until smooth. Beat in eggs, one at a time, then rind and juice. Pour evenly into paper cases.

4 Preheat a 4-hole (⅓-cup/80ml) pie maker. Place four cheesecakes into holes; refrigerate remaining cheesecakes until required. Close lid; cook for 8 minutes or until almost set, but slightly soft in the centre. Remove gently; transfer to a wire rack to cool completely. Repeat with remaining cheesecakes. Refrigerate cooled cheesecakes for 1 hour or until chilled.

5 Cut cheeks from mangoes. Using a large metal spoon, scoop to remove the cheek flesh in one piece; cut widthways into thin slices. Just before serving, arrange mango slices on top of cheesecakes, then decorate with blueberries, lemon rind strips and mint.

tip We used smooth-sided firm paper cases, cut down to fit in the pie maker; you can use any paper cases you like. Make sure the top of the cheesecakes do not come in contact with the pie maker lid.

sweet stuff

CHOCOLATE LAVA CAKES

**PREP + COOK TIME 30 MINUTES
MAKES 6**

ingredients

125g (4oz) butter, softened

⅔ cup (150g) firmly packed brown sugar

2 eggs

½ cup (75g) plain flour (all-purpose flour)

¼ cup (25g) cocoa powder, plus 2 teaspoons extra, to serve

1½ tablespoons milk

6 Lindt milk or hazelnut chocolate balls

thick (double) cream and extra crushed Lindt balls, to serve

1 Lightly grease and preheat a 4-hole (⅓-cup/80ml) pie maker.

2 Beat butter and sugar in a small bowl with an electric mixer until light and fluffy. Beat in eggs, one at a time. Stir in sifted flour, cocoa and milk.

3 Spoon ¼ cup mixture into prepared holes. Close lid; cook for 4 minutes or until partially cooked. Lightly push one Lindt ball into the middle of each cake; smooth surface to enclose the ball. Close lid; cook for another 4 minutes or until firm but slightly soft in the centre. Open lid; leave cakes in heated pie maker for a further 2 minutes. Gently remove cakes; turn onto serving plates. Repeat with remaining mixture and Lindt balls to make 6 cakes in total.

4 Serve lava cakes warm, topped with cream and extra Lindt balls; dust with extra cocoa.

LEMONADE JELLY CAKES

PREP + COOK TIME 30 MINUTES (+ COOLING & REFRIGERATION)
MAKES 8

ingredients

85g (3oz) packet raspberry jelly crystals

470g (15oz) packet vanilla cake mix (see tips)

1 cup (250ml) lemonade (see tips)

1½ cups (120g) desiccated coconut

½ cup (125ml) thickened cream (heavy cream)

1 Dissolve jelly crystals with 1 cup (250ml) boiling water in a large bowl; stir in ⅔ cup (180ml) cold water until combined. Refrigerate for 1 hour or until jelly is partially set (it should be thick and viscous like egg whites, but still stir-able).

2 Lightly grease and preheat a 4-hole (⅓-cup/80ml) pie maker.

3 Whisk cake mix and lemonade in a large bowl until smooth.

4 Pour ¼ cup of mixture into prepared holes. Close and cook for 7 minutes or until a skewer inserted into centre comes out clean. Gently transfer cakes to a wire rack to cool. Repeat with remaining mixture.

5 Place coconut in a bowl. Dip cooled cakes in jelly; drain off excess. Toss cakes in coconut. Place on a baking-paper-lined tray; refrigerate for 30 minutes or until set. (Return leftover jelly to the fridge until set; reserve for another use.)

6 Beat cream in a small bowl with an electric mixer until firm peaks form. Cut a 2cm (¾in) round from the top of each cake and spoon a little whipped cream into each hole.

tips Most packet cake mixes come with a ready-made icing, set this aside for another use. Use a clear, carbonated lemonade for this recipe.

CARROT CAKES

PREP + COOK TIME 35 MINUTES (+ COOLING) MAKES 6

ingredients

1 egg
½ cup (110g) firmly packed brown sugar
⅓ cup (80ml) vegetable oil
1 cup (120g) coarsely grated carrot
⅓ cup (40g) coarsely chopped walnuts
¾ cup (115g) self-raising flour
⅛ teaspoon bicarbonate of soda (baking soda)
¾ teaspoon mixed spice
2 tablespoons chopped walnuts, extra
2 tablespoons pure maple syrup

CREAM CHEESE FROSTING

100g (3oz) butter, softened
250g (8oz) cream cheese, softened
1 teaspoon vanilla extract
3½ cups (560g) icing sugar (confectioners' sugar)
1½ tablespoons pure maple syrup

1 Lightly grease and preheat a 4-hole (⅓-cup/80ml) pie maker.

2 Beat egg, sugar and oil in a small bowl with an electric mixer until thick and creamy. Transfer mixture to a large bowl; stir in carrot and walnuts, then sifted dry ingredients.

3 Spoon ¼ cup mixture into prepared holes. Close lid; cook for 7 minutes or until a skewer inserted into centre comes out clean. Gently remove; transfer to a wire rack to cool. Repeat with remaining mixture to make 6 cakes in total.

4 Meanwhile, to make frosting, beat butter, cream cheese and vanilla in a large bowl with electric mixer until fluffy. Gradually beat in sifted icing sugar, then maple syrup. Freeze for 10 minutes or until firm.

5 Spoon frosting into a large piping bag fitted with a 1cm (½in) star tube. Pipe generous swirls of frosting onto cold cakes. Just before serving, top with extra chopped walnuts and drizzle with maple syrup.

sweet stuff

VICTORIA SPONGE CAKES

PREP + COOK TIME 25 MINUTES (+ COOLING) MAKES 8

ingredients

125g (4oz) butter

½ teaspoon vanilla extract

½ cup (110g) caster sugar (superfine sugar)

2 eggs

2 tablespoons milk

1 cup (150g) self-raising flour

½ cup (125ml) thickened cream (heavy cream)

2 tablespoons strawberry jam

icing sugar (confectioners' sugar), to serve

1 Lightly grease and preheat a 4-hole (⅓-cup/80ml) pie maker.

2 Beat butter, vanilla and sugar in a small bowl with an electric mixer until light and fluffy (see tips). Beat in eggs, one at a time; beat in milk. Stir in sifted flour, in two batches, until smooth.

3 Spoon ¼ cup mixture into prepared holes. Close lid; cook for 8 minutes or until a skewer inserted into centre comes out clean. Gently transfer cakes to a wire rack to cool completely. Repeat with remaining mixture.

4 Meanwhile, beat cream in a small bowl with electric mixer until firm peaks form.

5 Split cooled cakes in half; sandwich together with jam and whipped cream. Serve dusted with sifted icing sugar.

tips Make sure you beat the butter, sugar and egg mixture thoroughly. These cakes are best eaten on the day they are made.

BOTTLED SAUCES

There is no easier way to pimp a sweet pie then to serve it with a delicious sauce, and, no we don't mean making one. Your pantry and fridge are probably already a good source (no pun intended) of an assortment of syrupy offerings to match your pies.

1 Chocolate sauce You can use chocolate ice-cream sauce, topping or Nutella thinned with a little hot water. For a chocolate peanut butter sauce, mix chocolate ice-cream sauce with smooth peanut butter.

2 Caramel sauce Ice-cream topping, thinned dulce de leche or caramel top 'n' fill are all options, with or without some crushed salt flakes. This universal flavour suits most sweet pies.

3 Vanilla custard Will work with most sweet pies and a lot of baked goods in the 'other stuff' chapter. If you want to play with the flavour, add a little finely grated orange or lemon rind or even mix with chocolate or caramel sauce.

4 Passionfruit Open a can of passionfruit pulp, use a bottled sauce or fresh pulp. Try with creamy flavours, chocolate, caramel and other fruits.

TRIPLE CHOC-CHUNK BROWNIES

PREP + COOK TIME 55 MINUTES (+ COOLING) MAKES 12

ingredients

125g (4oz) butter, chopped
200g (6½oz) dark (semi-sweet) chocolate, chopped coarsely
1 cup (220g) firmly packed brown sugar
2 eggs, beaten lightly
1 cup (150g) plain flour (all-purpose flour)
150g (4½oz) white chocolate, chopped coarsely
100g (3oz) milk chocolate, chopped coarsely

1 Place butter and dark chocolate in a medium saucepan; stir over low heat until almost smooth. Remove from heat; cool for 10 minutes. Stir sugar and egg into chocolate mixture, followed by sifted flour, then white and milk chocolate.

2 Preheat a 4-hole (⅓-cup/80ml) pie maker. With 24 (⅓-cup/80ml) paper cases, stack two together to create 12 double-layered cases; place cases on a tray, spray with oil. Spoon mixture evenly among cases.

3 Place four brownies into holes. Close lid; cook for 14 minutes or until just set to touch. Gently transfer to a wire rack to cool. Repeat in batches with remaining brownies.

4 Remove paper cases before serving, if you like.

CHOCOLATE CUPCAKES & STRAWBERRY BUTTERCREAM

PREP + COOK TIME 40 MINUTES (+ COOLING) MAKES 12

ingredients

1 cup (150g) self-raising flour
½ cup (75g) plain flour (all-purpose flour)
⅓ cup (35g) cocoa powder
1 teaspoon bicarbonate of soda (baking soda)
1 teaspoon baking powder
¼ teaspoon salt
¾ cup (165g) caster sugar (superfine sugar)
185g (6oz) butter, softened
3 eggs
½ cup (125ml) milk

STRAWBERRY BUTTERCREAM

300g (9½oz) butter, softened
2 x 250g (8oz) packets strawberry buttercream icing mix

1 Lightly grease and preheat a 4-hole (⅓-cup/80ml) pie maker.

2 Sift flours, cocoa, bicarb soda, baking powder and salt into a large bowl of an electric mixer, add sugar, butter, eggs and milk; beat on low speed until ingredients are combined. Increase speed to medium; beat until mixture is smooth and has changed to a paler colour.

3 Spoon ¼ cup mixture into prepared holes. Close lid; cook for 8 minutes or until a skewer inserted into centre comes out clean. Transfer to a wire rack to cool completely. Repeat in batches with remaining mixture to make 12 cakes in total.

4 To make strawberry buttercream, beat butter in a small bowl with electric mixer until pale and fluffy. Gradually beat in buttercream icing mix and 1½ tablespoons water; beat until smooth.

5 Spoon buttercream into a large piping bag fitted with a 1cm (½in) star tube. Pipe generous swirls of buttercream on top of cakes.

BANANA BREAD MUFFINS

PREP + COOK TIME 30 MINUTES
MAKES 8

ingredients

- 60g (2oz) butter, softened
- ½ cup (110g) firmly packed brown sugar
- ½ teaspoon vanilla extract
- 1 egg
- ¾ cups (200g) mashed ripe banana
- ¾ cup (110g) plain flour (all-purpose flour)
- ½ teaspoon bicarbonate of soda (baking soda)
- ½ teaspoon baking powder
- ½ teaspoon ground cinnamon
- ⅛ teaspoon salt flakes
- 2 tablespoons coarsely chopped roasted walnuts
- 8 dried banana chips

1 Beat butter, sugar and vanilla in a medium bowl with an electric mixer until paler and fluffy. Beat in egg, until just combined, then mashed banana. Sift flour, bicarb soda, baking powder, cinnamon and salt over mixture. Add walnuts; stir with a large spoon until combined.

2 LIghtly grease and preheat a 4-hole (⅓-cup/80ml) pie maker.

3 Spoon ¼ cup mixture into prepared holes. Close lid; cook for 4 minutes. Top each with a banana slice in centre. Close lid; cook for a further 4 minutes or until a skewer inserted into centre comes out clean. Gently remove; transfer to a wire rack. Repeat with remaining mixture and banana chips.

sweet stuff

BERRY CUSTARD CROISSANT PUDDINGS

PREP + COOK TIME 15 MINUTES (+ STANDING) MAKES 4

ingredients
6 small croissants (200g)
⅓ cup (160g) strawberry jam
CUSTARD
½ cup (125ml) pouring cream
2 tablespoons caster sugar (superfine sugar)
1 egg
1 teaspoon vanilla extract

1 To make custard, whisk cream, sugar, egg and vanilla in a large bowl until combined. Transfer custard to a jug.

2 Cut croissants in half horizontally. Roll croissants with a rolling pin to flatten to 5mm (¼in) thick. Reserve 4 croissant tops.

3 Grease a 4-hole (⅓-cup/80ml) pie maker. With pie maker turned off, line each hole with remaining croissant bases and tops, pressing into base and sides to create a pie cases. Trim excess; place off-cuts into croissant cases, then fill with 2-3 tablespoons custard on top. Stand for 5 minutes for croissants to soak up some of the custard.

4 Spoon 1 tablespoon strawberry jam on each pudding. Trim reserved croissant tops to fit top of pie holes. Place trimmings on jam and add tops. Turn pie maker on. Place a wooden spoon or other 2cm (¾in) object on the edge of the pie maker to keep the lid slightly ajar. Partially close lid; cook for 5 minutes. Close lid completely; cook for a further 5 minutes or until custard is just set.

5 Stand puddings for 5 minutes before serving warm.

STICKY DATE PUDDINGS

PREP + COOK TIME 40 MINUTES (+ STANDING) MAKES 10

ingredients

1½ cups (210g) dates, chopped coarsely

1 teaspoon bicarbonate of soda (baking soda)

60g (2oz) butter, softened

¾ cup (165g) firmly packed brown sugar

2 eggs, beaten lightly

1 cup (150g) self-raising flour

¼ cup (25g) finely chopped walnuts, plus extra to serve

¼ cup (25g) finely chopped pecans, plus extra to serve

vanilla ice-cream, to serve

CARAMEL SAUCE

1 cup (220g) firmly packed brown sugar

300ml pouring cream

100g (3oz) butter, chopped

1 Combine dates and 1 cup (250ml) boiling water in a medium heatproof bowl. Stir in bicarb soda; stand for 5 minutes.

2 Process date mixture with butter and sugar until smooth. Add eggs and sifted flour; process until just combined. Stir in walnuts and pecans; pour mixture into a large jug.

3 Lightly grease and preheat a 4-hole (⅓-cup/80ml) pie maker.

4 Pour ⅓ cup mixture into prepared holes. Close lid; cook for 7 minutes or until a skewer inserted into centre comes out clean. Gently remove; transfer to a wire rack. Repeat in batches with remaining mixture to make 10 puddings in total.

5 Meanwhile, to make caramel sauce, stir sugar, cream and butter in a medium saucepan over low-medium heat, without boiling, until sugar dissolves. Simmer, stirring, for 3 minutes.

6 Serve puddings warm topped with scoops of ice-cream, sauce and extra walnuts.

sweet stuff

SCONES

**PREP + COOK TIME 30 MINUTES
MAKES 8**

ingredients

1¼ cups (185g) self-raising flour
2 teaspoons caster sugar (superfine sugar)
⅛ teaspoon salt
15g (½oz) butter
⅔ cup (160ml) buttermilk, approximately
1 egg
2 tablespoons milk
jam and whipped cream, to serve

1 Sift flour, sugar and salt into a large bowl; rub in butter with your fingertips. Make a well in the centre; add buttermilk. Using a knife, 'cut' buttermilk through flour mixture to form a soft, sticky dough; add a little more buttermilk only if needed.

2 Gently knead dough on a floured surface until smooth. Using your hands, press dough out evenly until 2cm (¾in) thick. Cut into 5cm (2in) rounds with a floured cutter; place on a baking-paper-lined tray, then cover loosely with baking paper (to prevent drying out). Gently knead scraps of dough together; repeat pressing and cutting, to make a total of eight scones.

3 Lightly grease and preheat a 4-hole (⅓-cup/80ml) pie maker. Whisk egg and milk in a small bowl.

4 Place dough rounds into prepared holes; brush tops with egg wash. Close lid; cook for 8 minutes or until browned and scones sound hollow when tapped firmly on the top with your fingers. Gently remove; transfer to a wire rack. Repeat with remaining dough rounds and egg wash.

5 Serve scones warm with jam and whipped cream.

tip Scones are best eaten on the day they are made.

sweet stuff

HOT CROSS BUN SCONES

PREP + COOK TIME 50 MINUTES (+ STANDING) MAKES 12

ingredients
½ cup (80g) currants
1 tablespoon dark rum
1¾ cups (260g) self-raising flour
1½ teaspoons mixed spice
1 teaspoon ground cinnamon
½ cup (125ml) chilled lemonade (see tips)
½ cup (125ml) pouring cream
1 egg
2 tablespoons milk
1 tablespoon warmed honey
½ cup (80g) icing sugar (confectioner' sugar)
3 teaspoons lemon juice
butter, to serve

1 Combine currants and rum in a medium heatproof bowl. Cover; microwave on HIGH (100%) power for 1 minute.

2 Sift flour and spices into a large bowl. Make a well in the centre; add lemonade, cream and currant mixture. Use a knife to cut the liquid and currants through the mixture, mixing to a soft, sticky dough.

3 Gently knead dough on a floured surface until smooth. Using your hands, press dough out evenly until 2cm (¾in) thick. Cut into 5cm (2in) rounds with a floured cutter; place on a baking-paper-lined tray, then cover loosely with baking paper (to prevent drying out). Gently knead scraps of dough together; repeat pressing and cutting to make a total of 12 scones.

4 Lightly grease and preheat a 4-hole (⅓-cup/80ml) pie maker. Whisk egg and milk in a small bowl.

5 Place dough rounds into prepared holes; brush tops with egg wash. Close lid; cook for 7 minutes or until browned and scones sound hollow when tapped firmly on the top with your fingers. Gently remove; transfer to a wire rack, brush with honey. Repeat in batches with remaining dough rounds, egg wash and honey.

6 Combine sifted icing sugar and juice in a small bowl; spoon icing into a small piping bag fitted with a 5mm (¼in) plain tube. Pipe crosses onto cooled scones. Serve with butter.

tips Use a clear, carbonated lemonade for this recipe for a light-textured scone. Scones are best eaten on the day they are made.

MINI PAVLOVAS

PREP + COOK TIME 30 MINUTES (+ COOLING)
MAKES 4

ingredients

2 egg whites

½ cup (110g) caster sugar (superfine sugar)

1 teaspoon cornflour (cornstarch)

½ teaspoon white vinegar

½ cup (125ml) thickened cream (heavy cream)

4 strawberries (80g), hulled, quartered

15g (½oz) freeze-dried strawberries, crushed (optional)

1 Preheat a 4-hole (¾-cup/180ml) pie maker. With eight (⅓-cup/80ml) paper cases, stack two together to create four double-layered cases; place cases on a tray, smoothing out the pleats.

2 Whisk egg whites in a medium bowl with an electric mixer until soft peaks form. Gradually add sugar, beating until sugar has dissolved after each addition and mixture is thick and glossy. Beat in sifted cornflour, then vinegar, until just combined.

3 Spoon ⅓ cup of meringue mixture into paper cases; smooth surface so it won't touch the lid. Carefully place cases into pie maker, making sure the meringue doesn't touch the lid. Partially close lid, leaving it ajar by 7cm (2¾in) (place a heatproof object on the edge of the pie maker to keep the lid ajar); cook for 20 minutes or until dry to touch. Turn pie maker off; cool pavlovas in pie maker keeping the lid ajar.

4 Just before serving, beat cream in a small bowl with electric mixer until soft peaks form.

5 Spoon cream on pavlovas; top with fresh strawberries and sprinkle with freeze-dried strawberries.

tip Make sure that your bowl and whisk are clean and dry, as any fat or moisture will affect the volume you get from the egg whites.

sweet stuff

EIGHT-LAYER CELEBRATION CAKE

PREP
+ COOK
TIME
1 HOUR
10 MINUTES
(+ COOLING
& FREEZING)
SERVES
16

We used a family-size pie maker for this recipe.

ingredients

2 x 470g (15oz) packets chocolate cake mix (see tips)

1¼ cups (310ml) milk

125g (4oz) butter, softened

4 eggs

200g (6½oz) dark chocolate (70% cocoa), chopped coarsely

CHOCOLATE BUTTERCREAM

250g (8oz) butter, softened

2 x 250g (8oz) packets chocolate buttercream icing mix

1 Lightly grease and preheat a family-size (2½-cup/625ml) pie maker. Cover two wire racks with baking paper.

2 Beat cake mixes, milk, butter and eggs in a large bowl with an electric mixer on low speed, until combined. Increase speed to high; beat until smooth. Divide mixture into eight ⅔ cup (160ml) portions.

3 Pour one portion of mixture into pie maker; spread and smooth. Close lid; cook for 5 minutes or until a skewer inserted into centre comes out clean. Remove cake, turning top-side down (this helps to flatten the cake), onto wire rack to cool. Repeat with remaining mixture to make a total of eight cakes; re-grease pie maker as needed.

4 Meanwhile, to make chocolate buttercream, beat butter in a large bowl with an electric mixer until light and fluffy. Gradually add icing mix and 1½ tablespoons water, beat for 5 minutes or until smooth. Reserve one-third of the buttercream to cover sides and top of cake.

5 To assemble, place one cake onto a plate; spread with one-eighth of the buttercream, then top with another cake. Continue layering, finishing with an un-iced cake. Spread most of the reserved buttercream around the side with a palette knife to neaten. Insert three trimmed wooden skewers into the centre of the cake for support. Spread remaining buttercream on top of cake. Freeze for 30 minutes or until firm.

6 Melt chocolate in a small heatproof bowl over a small pan of simmering water (make sure the water doesn't touch the base of the bowl). Cool to a pouring consistency.

7 Pour cooled chocolate over chilled cake, allowing it to run down the side. Stand until set.

tips Most packet cake mixes come with an icing mix, set this aside for another use. Cool two cakes on each rack; when cool, move them on the paper to a flat surface to free up the racks. Stack cooled cakes.

THE OTHER STUFF

the other stuff

LASAGNE

PREP + COOK TIME 20 MINUTES (+ STANDING) MAKES 4

ingredients

375g (12oz) packet fresh lasagne sheets (see tips)

425g (13½oz) tub fresh beef bolognese pasta sauce

½ cup (60g) grated cheddar

½ cup (40g) finely grated parmesan, plus extra to serve

basil leaves, to serve

CHEAT'S BÉCHAMEL

1 cup (240g) smooth ricotta

¼ cup (60ml) thickened cream (heavy cream)

1 egg, beaten lightly

1 Lightly grease a 4-hole (¾-cup/180ml) pie maker.

2 Place four lasagne sheets on a work surface. Using pastry cutter provided as a stencil, mark four large rounds (15.5cm/6¼in) and four small rounds (12cm/4¾in) on lasagne sheets; cut out with scissors. Cut 12 x 8cm (3¼in) squares from remaining lasagne sheets. Cover and refrigerate until required.

3 To make the cheat's béchamel, whisk ricotta, cream and egg in a medium bowl until smooth.

4 With pie maker turned off, line prepared holes with large lasagne rounds; press into base and side, making sure there are no gaps. Spread 1 tablespoon béchamel and 1 tablespoon bolognese on each base, then sprinkle each with 3 teaspoons of combined cheeses; top with a lasagne square. Repeat layering two more times. Spread another 1 tablespoon bolognese on each to cover lasagne square. Be careful not to overfill or filling with bubble over. Top with small lasagne rounds and press edges firmly to seal; sprinkle with remaining cheeses and spray with oil.

5 Turn on pie maker. Close lid; cook lasagne for 8 minutes or until browned. Carefully remove; stand for 5 minutes before serving.

6 Serve lasagne topped with fresh basil leaves and extra parmesan.

tips We used 7 fresh lasagne sheets measuring 15.5cm x 29.5cm (6¼in x 12in); if you buy smaller sheets, you will need more. Freeze any leftover lasagne sheets and bolognese sauce for up to 2 months.

SAUSAGE ROLLS

PREP + COOK TIME 1 HOUR 15 MINUTES
MAKES 14

ingredients

3 gourmet pork sausages (250g)
3 gourmet beef sausages (250g)
1 small onion (80g), chopped finely
¼ cup (15g) stale breadcrumbs
1 egg yolk
2 teaspoons tomato paste
2 teaspoons barbecue sauce
1 tablespoon finely chopped fresh flat-leaf parsley
1 egg, beaten lightly
1 tablespoon milk
1 tablespoon sesame seeds
tomato sauce (ketchup), to serve

QUICK DOUGH

2 cups (300g) self-raising flour
½ teaspoon bicarbonate of soda (baking soda)
1 teaspoon salt
50g (1½oz) chilled butter, chopped
¾ cup (180ml) buttermilk, approximately

1 Cut a slit at the top of each sausage and squeeze out sausage meat from casing.

2 Combine sausage meat, onion, breadcrumbs, egg yolk, paste, sauce and parsley in a large bowl.

3 To make quick dough, sift flour, bicarb soda and salt into a medium bowl; using fingertips, rub butter into flour until mixture resembles coarse crumbs. Add enough buttermilk to form a soft, sticky dough. Turn dough onto a floured surface; knead gently until smooth. Roll dough into a 30cm x 40cm (12in x 16in) rectangle; cut in half lengthways.

4 Place equal amounts of the sausage mixture lengthways along the centre of each dough piece; roll up tightly, from long side, to enclose filling. Using a serrated knife, trim end of rolls, then cut each roll into seven 5cm (2in) pieces; place rolls, seam-side down, on trays.

5 Combine egg and milk in a small bowl. Brush rolls with egg wash; sprinkle with sesame seeds. Cover; refrigerate until required.

6 Lightly grease and preheat a 4-hole (⅓-cup/80ml) pie maker.

7 Place four sausage rolls, seam-side down, into prepared holes. Close lid; cook for 8 minutes or until golden. Carefully turn sausage rolls over, close lid; cook for a further 4 minutes or until cooked through. Transfer to a wire rack. Wipe holes clean with paper towel; re-grease as required. Repeat with remaining sausage rolls.

8 Serve sausage rolls warm with tomato sauce.

tips Use all pork or all beef sausages, if you prefer. To make breadcrumbs, process day-old bread in batches. Cooked sausage rolls can be frozen for up to 3 months. Reheat in the pie make for 8 minutes each side from frozen.

the other stuff

CHEESEBURGER PIES

PREP + COOK TIME 20 MINUTES MAKES 4

ingredients

4 sheets frozen shortcrust pastry, thawed
4 sesame hamburger buns (360g)
4 beef burger patties (330g)
8 cheddar sandwich slices (160g)
⅓ cup (70g) drained sliced bread and butter pickles
⅓ cup (95g) tomato sauce (ketchup)
2 tablespoons american mustard
½ cup (160g) caramelised onion
hot fries, to serve

1 Using pastry cutter provided for a 4-hole (¾-cup/180ml) pie maker, cut four large (15.5cm/6¼in) rounds from pastry. Refrigerate until required.

2 Split hamburger buns in half; reserve bottom halves for another use (see tip).

3 Grease and preheat a 4-hole (¾-cup/180ml) pie maker.

4 Place patties in prepared holes and press down with the back of a spoon to spread to edges. Close lid; cook for 3 minutes or until starting to brown around edges. Turn patties over, close lid; cook for a further 3 minutes or until cooked through. Remove; drain on paper towel.

5 Wipe holes clean with paper towel. Line prepared holes with shortcrust pastry rounds; carefully press into base and sides. Prick base of pie cases well with a fork. Close lid; cook for 3 minutes or until pastry is light golden.

6 Place patties inside pastry cases; top with a slice of cheddar, pickles, tomato sauce, mustard, another slice of cheddar, caramelised onion and the burger bun top. Partially close lid, keeping it held ajar by 3.5cm (1½in), taking care not to flatten burger bun top. Cook for 6 minutes or until pastry is cooked and burger is heated through.

7 Serve cheeseburger pies straightaway with hot fries.

tip You can use the burger bun bases to make breadcrumbs.

SPAGHETTI BOLOGNESE MUFFINS

PREP + COOK TIME 35 MINUTES
MAKES 10

ingredients

150g (4½oz) spaghetti

425g (13½oz) tub fresh beef bolognese pasta sauce

2 eggs, beaten lightly

⅓ cup (50g) plain flour (all-purpose flour)

⅓ cup finely chopped basil leaves

1 cup (120g) grated cheddar

¼ cup (20g) finely grated parmesan

10 cherry bocconcini (100g), halved

extra basil or oregano leaves, to serve

1 Break spaghetti in half; cook in a large saucepan of boiling salted water for 8 minutes or until tender. Drain; return to pan.

2 Add bolognese sauce to pasta; stir until well combined. Stir in egg, flour, basil and half the cheddar. Season with salt and pepper.

3 Combine remaining cheddar and parmesan in a small bowl.

4 Lightly grease and preheat a 4-hole (⅓-cup/80ml) pie maker.

5 Spoon ⅓ cup spaghetti mixture into holes, place a bocconcini on top of each and press down. Sprinkle with 1 tablespoon combined grated cheeses; spray with oil. Close lid; cook for 8-10 minutes or until muffins are firm and golden. Gently remove; transfer to a wire rack covered with baking paper, to cool. Wipe holes clean with paper towel; lightly grease. Repeat in batches with remaining spaghetti mixture, bocconcini and grated cheeses to make 10 muffins in total.

6 Serve warm or cold, topped with extra basil or oregano.

LAMB KOFTA & HALOUMI WRAPS

PREP + COOK TIME 25 MINUTES
MAKES 2

ingredients

250g (8oz) minced (ground) lamb
1 tablespoon fresh thyme leaves
1 tablespoon ground cumin
1 tablespoon ground sumac
½ teaspoon freshly ground black pepper
¼ teaspoon chilli powder
90g (3oz) haloumi, cut into four 5mm (¼in) thick slices
2 wholemeal lebanease breads
½ cup (135g) tzatziki dip, plus extra to serve
40g (1½oz) mixed salad leaves
⅓ cup fresh mint leaves, torn
¼ small red onion (25g), sliced thinly

1 Combine lamb, thyme, cumin, sumac, pepper and chilli in a medium bowl; season with salt. Using hands, mix thoroughly until well combined. Divide lamb mixture into eight equal portions and shape into balls.

2 Lightly grease and preheat a 4-hole (⅓-cup/80ml) pie maker.

3 Place one kofta into each prepared hole; close lid, cook for 4 minutes. Turn koftas, close lid; cook for a further 2 minutes or until browned and cooked through. Remove; drain on paper towel. Wipe holes clean with paper towel. Repeat with remaining koftas.

4 Place a haloumi slice into each prepared hole; close lid, cook for 3 minutes. Turn haloumi, close lid; cook for a further 2 minutes or until browned.

5 Spread lebanese bread with tzatziki; top with salad leaves, mint, onion, koftas and haloumi. Serve topped with extra tzatziki.

CHICKEN QUESADILLAS WITH AVOCADO CREAM

PREP + COOK TIME 35 MINUTES
MAKES 2

We used a family-size pie maker for this recipe.

ingredients

1.2kg (2½lb) whole roast or barbecued chicken
4 x 20cm (8in) large flour tortillas
½ cup (130g) chunky salsa
2 tablespoons sour cream
1½ cups (180g) grated cheddar
lime wedges, to serve

AVOCADO CREAM

1 medium avocado (250g), chopped
¼ cup (60g) sour cream
⅓ cup fresh coriander (cilantro) leaves
2 tablespoons lime juice
½ small clove garlic, crushed

1 Lightly grease and preheat a family-size (2½-cup/625ml) pie maker. Cut four 16cm x 50cm (6½in x 20in) pieces of baking paper.

2 Remove breast meat from chicken and shred coarsely; you need 2 cups shredded chicken. Reserve legs and wings for another use.

3 Place one piece of baking paper on a work surface. Spray one side of a tortilla with oil; place oil-side down in centre. Spread with half each of the salsa, shredded chicken, sour cream and cheddar. Top with another tortilla; press down firmly and spray with oil. Repeat with another pie of baking paper, then remaining tortillas, salsa, shredded chicken, sour cream and cheddar.

4 Using the baking paper for support, lift one quesadilla into pie maker. Close lid; cook for 7 minutes or until browned underneath. Gently lift quesadilla out of pie maker. Place another piece of baking paper on top; flip quesadilla over and return to pie maker. Close lid; cook for a further 5 minutes or until browned and heated through. Transfer to a plate; keep warm. Repeat with remaining quesadilla.

5 Meanwhile, to make avocado cream, process avocado, sour cream, coriander, lime juice and garlic in a small food processor until smooth. Season to taste.

6 Cut quesadillas into wedges and serve with avocado cream and lime wedges.

the other stuff

HAM & PINEAPPLE MINI PIZZAS

PREP + COOK TIME 40 MINUTES
MAKES 12

ingredients
200g (6½oz) pizza base (see tip)
¼ cup (70g) pizza sauce
1½ cups (150g) pizza cheese
80g (2½oz) shaved honey ham, cut into thin strips
100g (3oz) drained canned pineapple pieces, patted dry with paper towel
1½ tablespoons pizza cheese, extra
micro herbs, to serve

1 Lightly grease and preheat a 4-hole (⅓-cup/80ml) pie maker. Cut twelve 6cm x 15cm (2½in x 6in) pieces of baking paper.

2 Using a 6cm (2½in) round cutter, cut 12 rounds from pizza base.

3 Place the pieces of baking paper on a work surface; top with pizza rounds in the centre of each piece. Spread each round with 1 teaspoon pizza sauce. Top pizzas evenly with cheese, ham and pineapple. Using the baking paper for support, lift four of the pizzas into prepared holes; sprinkle with extra cheese.

4 Close lid; cook pizzas for 8-10 minutes or until cheese is golden brown and pizza bases are crisp. Remove; transfer to a wire rack lined with baking paper. Repeat in batches with remaining pizzas.

5 Serve topped with micro herbs.

tip We used a 26cm (10½in) pizza base. You could also use large flour tortilla or pitta breads instead.

BIG "THE WORKS" PIZZA

PREP + COOK TIME 20 MINUTES
MAKES 1

We used a family-size pie maker for this recipe.

ingredients

200g (6½oz) pizza base
2 tablespoons pizza sauce
8 pepperoni slices (20g)
3 salami slices (20g), torn
1 slice rindless shortcut bacon (35g), chopped
2 button mushrooms, sliced thinly
¼ small red capsicum (bell pepper) (50g), sliced thinly
¼ small red onion (25g), sliced thinly
4 grape tomatoes, halved
4 pitted kalamata olives
⅓ cup (35g) pizza cheese
soft herb of choice, to serve (see tip)

1 Lightly grease and preheat a family-size (2½-cup/625ml) pie maker. Cut a 12cm x 40cm (4¾in x 16in) piece of baking paper.

2 Using scissors, trim pizza base 2cm (¾in) wider than the base of pie maker hole (about 18cm/7¼in).

3 Place baking paper on a work surface; top with pizza base in the centre. Spread base with pizza sauce and top with pepperoni, salami, bacon, mushrooms, capsicum, onion, tomato and olives. Using the baking paper for support, lift pizza into pie maker; sprinkle with pizza cheese. Close lid; cook pizza for 12 minutes or until edges and cheese are golden brown.

4 Serve pizza topped with herbs.

tip Fresh basil and oreagno leaves would be a tasty addition to this pizza but you could also use flat-leaf parsley, if you prefer.

the other stuff

PIZZA SCROLLS

**PREP + COOK TIME 40 MINUTES
MAKES 12**

ingredients

2 cups (300g) self-raising flour

½ teaspoon bicarbonate of soda (baking soda)

1 teaspoon salt

50g (1½oz) cold butter, chopped

¾ cup (180ml) buttermilk, approximately

2 tablespoons pizza sauce

1 tablespoon barbecue pizza sauce (or barbecue sauce)

80g (2½oz) sliced pepperoni, chopped coarsely

½ small red onion (50g), sliced thinly

½ cup (55g) pitted kalamata olives, chopped coarsely

1 cup (100g) pizza cheese

fresh oregano leaves, to serve

1 Sift flour, bicarb soda and salt into a medium bowl; using fingertips, rub butter into flour until mixture resembles coarse crumbs. Add enough buttermilk to mix to a soft, sticky dough. Turn out dough onto a floured surface; knead gently until smooth. Roll dough into a 30cm x 40cm (12in x 16in) rectangle.

2 Lightly grease and preheat a 4-hole (⅓-cup/80ml) pie maker. Cut 12 x 6cm x 15cm (2½in x 6in) pieces of baking paper; line holes with four pieces of paper.

3 Spread dough with combined sauces; sprinkle with pepperoni, onion, olives and pizza cheese, leaving a 3cm (1¼in) gap along the top edge. Roll up dough tightly from long side; pinch seam to seal. Using a serrated knife, trim ends. Cut roll into 12 x 3cm (1¼in) thick slices.

4 Place four scrolls, cut-side down, into prepared holes; spray with oil. Close lid; cook for 8 minutes or until risen and pastry is golden. Remove; transfer to a wire rack to cool. Repeat in batches with remaining paper and scrolls.

5 Serve scrolls topped with fresh oregano.

PROSCIUTTO EGG CUPS

PREP + COOK TIME 15 MINUTES
MAKES 4

ingredients
8 slices prosciutto (100g)
4 eggs
2 slices swiss cheese (12g), halved
chopped fresh flat-leaf parsley, to serve

1 Lightly grease a 4-hole (⅓-cup/80ml) pie maker. Cut four 6cm x 15cm (2½in x 6in) pieces of baking paper; line holes with paper.

2 With pie maker turned off, line each prepared hole with two slices of prosciutto, overlapping slightly; press into base and side, making sure there are no gaps. Trim excess with scissors, add to prosciutto cases. Line prosciutto cases with cheese. Crack an egg on top.

3 Turn on pie maker. Close lid; cook for 9 minutes or until the white of the egg is cooked but the yolk remains runny. Using the baking paper for support, carefully remove prosciutto egg cups. Season to taste. Serve straightaway topped with parsley.

MINI HOT DOGS

PREP
+ COOK
TIME
35 MINUTES
(+ STANDING)
MAKES
12

ingredients

12 cocktail frankfurts (300g)
¾ cup (90g) grated cheddar
tomato sauce (ketchup) and american mustard, to serve

QUICK DOUGH

1 cup (150g) self-raising flour
¼ teaspoon bicarbonate of soda (baking soda)
½ teaspoon salt
25g (¾oz) cold butter, chopped
⅓ cup (80ml) buttermilk, approximately

1 To make quick dough, sift flour, bicarb soda and salt into a medium bowl; using fingertips, rub butter into flour until mixture resembles coarse crumbs. Add enough buttermilk to mix to a soft, sticky dough. Turn out dough onto a floured surface; knead gently until smooth. Roll dough into a 20cm x 36cm (8in x 14½in) rectangle, with the long edge facing you (use a ruler to help straighten up the edges). Cut dough in half lengthways, then cut each rectangle into six 6cm x 10cm (2½in x 4in) pieces to make a total of 12 pieces. Cover until ready to use.

2 Place frankfurts in a large bowl, cover with boiling water and stand for 5 minutes; drain and pat dry with paper towel.

3 Lightly grease and preheat a 4-hole (⅓-cup/80ml) pie maker. Cut 12 x 6cm x 15cm (2½in x 6in) pieces of baking paper.

4 Place pieces of baking paper on a work surface; top with dough pieces in the centre. Sprinkle evenly with grated cheese and lay a frankfurt crossways in the centre. Bring short sides of dough up over frankfurt to almost meet at the top, leaving a 5mm (¼in) gap. Using the baking paper for support, gently lift four hot dogs into prepared holes.

5 Close lid; cook hot dogs, for 8 minutes or until pastry is puffed and golden. Remove; transfer to a wire rack to cool. Repeat in batches with remaining hot dogs.

6 Serve hot dogs topped with tomato sauce and mustard.

BACHELOR'S BIG BREAKFAST

PREP + COOK TIME 10 MINUTES
SERVES 1

ingredients

1 slice white bread
⅓ cup (90g) baked beans
½ medium tomato (75g)
2 slices rindless shortcut bacon (70g)
1 egg
toast and tomato sauce (ketchup), to serve

1 Lightly grease and preheat a 4-hole (⅓-cup/80ml) pie maker.

2 Roughly trim crusts from bread and discard; roll slice with a rolling pin to flatten to 5mm (¼in) thick. Line a prepared hole with bread slice; carefully press into base and side. Spoon baked beans into bread case.

3 Place tomato, cut-side up, in another hole; season with freshly ground black pepper.

4 Place a bacon slice in each of the remaining holes.

5 Close lid; cook breakfast for 4 minutes. Remove one of the slices of bacon and place it in with the other slice. Crack an egg into the empty hole. Close lid; cook for a further 3 minutes or until the yolk is cooked to your liking.

6 Serve the big breakfast with toast and tomato sauce.

the other stuff

REUBEN TOASTIE

**PREP + COOK TIME 15 MINUTES
MAKES 4**

ingredients
8 slices rye bread
8 slices pastrami (130g)
8 slices swiss cheese (160g), halved
⅓ cup (50g) drained sauerkraut
cooking oil spray
pickles, to serve
RUSSIAN DRESSING
¼ cup (75g) whole-egg mayonnaise
2 teaspoons sriracha (chilli sauce)
1 teaspoon horseradish cream
½ teaspoon worcestershire sauce

1 Lightly grease and preheat a 4-hole (⅓-cup/80ml) pie maker.

2 To make russian dressing, stir ingredients together in a small bowl.

3 Roughly trim crusts from bread and discard; roll slices with a rolling pin to flatten to 3mm (⅛in) thick. Line prepared holes with four thin slices of bread; press into base and side.

4 Fold pastrami slices into quarters; place two in each bread case. Top each one with a slice of cheese, a quarter of the sauerkraut, 1 teaspoon russian dressing and another slice of cheese. Top with remaining bread slices; the bread will extend over the top. Close lid to seal the edges, then immediately open again. Spray tops of pies with oil. Close lid; cook toasties for 7 minutes or until bread is toasted and cheese is melted.

5 Serve toasties with remaining dressing and pickles.

BIG SPINACH COB

PREP + COOK TIME 30 MINUTES
SERVES 8

We used a family-size pie maker for this recipe.

ingredients

1 x 18cm (7¼in) sourdough cob loaf
cooking oil spray
250g (8oz) frozen spinach, thawed
1¼ cups (300g) sour cream
½ cup (60g) grated cheddar
40g (1½oz) packet french onion soup mix

1 Lightly grease and preheat a family-size (2½-cup/625ml) pie maker.

2 Slice the top from the cob loaf, making sure the base is about 4cm (1½in) high. Neatly cut out the bread centre, as one piece, leaving a 1.5cm (¾in) border; reserve.

3 Spray both sides of bread centre with oil and place in pie maker. Hold lid adjar by 3cm (1¼cm), so the top of the lid does not come in contact with the loaf. Cook cob for 5 minutes or until bread is golden and crisp. Remove and keep warm.

4 Spray both sides of cob loaf top with oil and place in pie maker. Close lid; cook for 5 minutes or until golden. Remove from pie maker; cover to keep warm.

5 Meanwhile, squeeze out excess water from thawed spinach. Combine spinach, sour cream, cheddar and soup mix in a large bowl.

6 Return cob loaf to pie maker; spoon in spinach mixture. Hold lid adjar by 3cm (1¼cm), so the top of the lid does not come in contact with the loaf. Cook for 10 minutes or until bread is browned and filling is heated through.

7 Just before serving, stir dip. Serve cob dip with reserved bread centre and cob loaf top, torn into pieces.

the other stuff

ASIAN FISH CAKES WITH CHILLI-MAYO DIPPING SAUCE

PREP + COOK TIME 55 MINUTES
MAKES 12

ingredients

150g (4½oz) hot smoked salmon fillet, skin removed

½ cup (125g) store-bought mashed potato

1 tablespoon thai red curry paste

2 green onions (scallions), sliced thinly

1 tablespoon finely chopped thai basil or fresh coriander (cilantro) leaves, plus extra to serve

1 egg, beaten lightly

1¼ cups (95g) panko (japanese) breadcrumbs

cooking oil spray

red chilli, green onion and lime wedges, to serve

CHILLI-MAYO DIPPING SAUCE

½ cup (75g) japanese (kewpie) mayonnaise

1 tablespoon sriracha (chilli sauce)

1 Flake salmon into a medium bowl; mash with a folk into smaller pieces. Add mashed potato, curry paste, green onion, coriander, egg and ¾ cup (55g) breadcrumbs; stir well to combine. Divide mixture into 12 portions and shape into 6cm (2½in) patties.

2 Place remaining breadcrumbs in a shallow bowl; coat patties gently in breadcrumbs.

3 Grease and preheat a 4-hole (⅓-cup/80ml) pie maker.

4 Place four fish cakes in prepared holes. Close lid; cook for 7 minutes or until starting to brown. Spray fish cakes with oil; gently turn over. Close lid; cook for another 7 minutes or until golden brown on both sides. Remove; transfer to a wire rack lined with baking paper. Repeat in batches with remaining fish cakes.

5 To make chilli-mayo dipping sauce, combine mayonnaise and sriracha in a small bowl.

6 Serve fish cakes with dipping sauce, chilli, green onion, extra herbs and lime wedges,

MAC 'N' CHEESE

PREP + COOK TIME 50 MINUTES (+ COOLING)
MAKES 12

ingredients

- 205g (6½oz) packet mac & cheese (see tip)
- ½ cup (125ml) milk
- 80g (2½oz) butter, chopped
- 100g (3oz) sliced ham, chopped finely
- ½ cup (60g) grated cheddar
- ⅓ cup (80g) sour cream
- 2 eggs, beaten lightly
- 1 cup (70g) panko (japanese) breadcrumbs
- ½ cup (40g) finely grated parmesan
- 1 tablespoon fresh thyme leaves

1 Cook pasta in a medium saucepan of boiling salted water for 10 minutes or until tender. Drain, do not rinse; return pasta to pan.

2 Add milk, 40g (1½oz) of the butter and the dried sauce sachet; stir to combine. Cook for 3-4 minutes over medium heat or until sauce thickens, stirring regularly. Add ham, cheddar and 2 tablespoons sour cream; stir until melted and combined. Remove from heat, stand to cool slightly; stir in egg.

3 Combine breadcrumbs, parmesan and thyme in a small bowl. Season with salt and pepper.

4 Lightly grease and preheat a 4-hole (⅓-cup/80ml) pie maker.

5 Spoon 2 tablespoons macaroni mixture into prepared holes, top each with 2 teaspoons sour cream and another 2 tablespoons macaroni mixture. Sprinkle with 2 tablespoons breadcrumb mixture; dot tops with remaining 40g (1½oz) butter.

6 Close lid; cook mac and cheese for 8-10 minutes or until golden and set. Gently remove; transfer to a wire rack covered with baking paper. Wipe holes clean with paper towel. Repeat in batches with remaining macaroni mixture to make 12 in total.

tip We used an instant mac and cheese packet that included the macaroni pasta and a sachet of dried cheese sauce.

SPRING QUICHES

PREP + COOK TIME 30 MINUTES
MAKES 8

ingredients

2 sheets frozen shortcrust pastry, thawed

2 eggs

¼ cup (60ml) thickened cream (heavy cream)

¼ cup (60g) soft ricotta, plus 2 tablespoons, extra

⅓ cup (25g) finely grated parmesan

2 tablespoons finely chopped dill, plus extra to serve

1 teaspoon finely grated lemon rind, plus extra to serve

170g (5½oz) asparagus, trimmed, halved lengthways, cut into 5cm (2in) lengths

1 medium zucchini (120g), cut into ribbons

1 Using pastry cutter provided for a 4-hole (⅓-cup/80ml) pie maker, cut eight large rounds (11cm/4½in) from shortcrust pastry. Refrigerate until required.

2 To make filling, whisk eggs, cream and ricotta in a large jug. Stir in parmesan, dill and lemon rind. Season with salt and pepper.

3 Lightly grease a 4-hole (⅓-cup/80ml) pie maker. With pie maker turned off, line prepared holes with pastry rounds; press into base and side.

4 Reserve eight asparagus tips. Divide half each of the remaining asparagus and the zucchini into pastry cases. Top each with 2 tablespoons filling, 1 teaspoon of the extra ricotta and a reserved asparagus tip.

5 Turn on pie maker. Close lid; cook for 10 minutes or until top is golden and egg is set. Gently remove; transfer to a wire rack. Repeat with remaining pastry rounds, vegetables, filling, extra ricotta and reserved asparagus tips.

6 Serve quiches topped with extra dill and lemon rind.

SPINACH & THREE CHEESE MUFFINS

PREP + COOK TIME 25 MINUTES
MAKES 10

ingredients
- 2 tablespoons olive oil
- 1 small onion (80g), chopped finely
- 100g (3oz) baby spinach leaves
- 80g (2½oz) butter, melted
- 1 egg
- 1 cup (250ml) buttermilk
- 2 cups (300g) self-raising flour
- ½ cup (50g) coarsely grated mozzarella
- ½ cup (40g) coarsely grated parmesan
- 100g (3oz) blue cheese, crumbled (see tip)

1 Heat oil in a medium frying pan over medium heat; cook onion, stirring, for 5 minutes or until softened. Add spinach; cook, stirring for 1 minute or until wilted. Cool.

2 Lightly grease and preheat a 4-hole (⅓-cup/80ml) pie maker.

3 Whisk butter, egg and buttermilk together in a jug. Sift flour into a large bowl; pour in wet ingredients, stir gently to combine. Add spinach mixture and all cheeses; stir gently to combine. Do not over mix; mixture should be lumpy.

4 Spoon heaped ⅓ cup of mixture into prepared holes. Close lid; cook for 6 minutes or until golden and a skewer inserted into the centre comes out clean. Gently remove; transfer to a wire rack. Wipe holes clean with paper towel. Repeat in batches with remaining mixture to make 10 muffins in total.

tip If you do not like blue cheese, use double the quantity of one of the other cheeses.

the other stuff

CORN FRITTERS

PREP + COOK TIME 25 MINUTES
MAKES 8

ingredients

420g (13½oz) can corn kernels, drained, rinsed
¾ cup (110g) self-raising flour
2 green onions (scallions), sliced thinly
2 eggs
⅓ cup (80ml) milk
cooking oil spray
¼ cup baby rocket (arugula) leaves
1 small avocado (200g), cut into wedges
¼ cup (60ml) sweet chilli sauce

1 Grease and preheat a 4-hole (¾-cup/180ml) pie maker.

2 Combine corn, flour and green onions in a large bowl.

3 Whisk eggs and milk together in a small jug. Add to corn mixture; stir until combined.

4 Spoon ¼ cup of batter into prepared holes (see tip); spread and smooth surface with the back of a spoon. Close lid; cook for 5 minutes or until almost set. Spray fritters with oil; turn over fritters. Close lid; cook for a further 5 minutes or until golden brown. Transfer fritters to a plate; cover to keep warm. Repeat with remaining mixture.

5 Serve fritters topped with rocket, avocado and sweet chilli sauce.

tip To make 12 small fritters, if using a 4-hole (⅓-cup/80ml) pie maker, spoon 1 tablespoon batter into prepared holes and continue with the recipe as directed.

HALOUMI, HARISSA & HONEY BRIOCHE SLIDERS

PREP
+ COOK
TIME
30 MINUTES
MAKES
4

ingredients

2 x 180g (5½oz) packets haloumi
plain (all-purpose) flour, for dusting
4 brioche slider buns, split
2 teaspoons harissa paste (see tip)
1 tablespoon honey
mixed salad leaves, to serve

1 Grease and preheat a 4-hole (⅓-cup/80ml) pie maker.

2 Drain haloumi; pat dry with paper towel. Cut each block of haloumi into quarters to make eight 4.5cm (1¾in) squares.

3 Dust haloumi squares in flour, shaking off excess; place in prepared holes. Close lid; cook for 7 minutes. Turn haloumi; close lid, cook for a further 7 minutes or until browned. Remove and drain on paper towel. Repeat with remaining haloumi.

4 Spread each slider base with harissa; place cut-side down, into holes. Close lid; cook for 3 minutes or until warmed through and golden. Remove; top each base with two pieces of haloumi and drizzle with honey. Top with salad leaves and slider tops. Serve straightaway.

tip You can use sriracha sauce instead of the harissa if you prefer.

GLOSSARY

ALMONDS
flaked paper-thin slices.
meal also known as ground almonds; powdered to a coarse flour-like texture.
BACON also known as bacon slices or rashers.
BAKING PAPER also called parchment or baking parchment; a silicone-coated paper that is primarily used for lining baking pans and oven trays so cooked food doesn't stick, making removal easy.
BAKING POWDER a raising agent consisting mainly of two parts cream of tartar to one part bicarbonate of soda (baking soda).
BASIL, SWEET the most common type of basil; this herb is used extensively in Italian dishes and is one of the main ingredients in pesto.
BAY LEAVES aromatic leaves from the bay tree, sold fresh or dried; adds a strong, slightly peppery flavour.
BEEF
eye-fillet tenderloin, fillet; fine texture, most expensive and extremely tender.
minced also known as ground beef.
BICARBONATE OF SODA (BAKING SODA) a mild alkali used as a raising agent in baking.
BREADCRUMBS
panko (japanese) are available in two kinds: larger pieces and fine crumbs; have a lighter texture than Western-style ones. Available from Asian food stores and most supermarkets.
stale crumbs made by grating, blending or processing 1- or 2-day-old bread.
BUTTER we use salted butter unless stated otherwise; 125g is equal to 1 stick (4oz). Unsalted or 'sweet' butter has no salt added and is popular butter among pastry chefs.
BUTTERMILK originally the term given to the slightly sour liquid left after butter was churned from cream, today it is made from no-fat or low-fat milk to which specific bacterial cultures have been added.
CAPSICUM (BELL PEPPER) comes in many colours: red, green, yellow and orange. Discard seeds and membranes before use.
CHEESE
bocconcini from the diminutive of 'boccone', meaning mouthful in Italian; walnut-sized, baby mozzarella, a delicate, semi-soft, white cheese traditionally made from buffalo milk. Sold fresh, it spoils rapidly; keep, refrigerated in brine, for 1 or 2 days at the most.
brie soft-ripened cow-milk cheese with a delicate, creamy texture and a rich, sweet taste that varies from buttery to mushroomy. Best served at room temperature after a brief period of ageing, brie should have a bloomy white rind and creamy, voluptuous centre which becomes runny with ripening.
cheddar the most common cow's milk 'tasty' cheese; should be aged, hard and have a pronounced bite.
cream commonly called philadelphia or philly; a soft cow-milk cheese, its fat content ranges from 14 to 33%.
goat's made from goat's milk, has an earthy, strong taste; available in soft and firm textures, in various shapes and sizes, and sometimes rolled in ash or herbs.
haloumi a Greek Cypriot cheese with a semi-firm, spongy texture and very salty sweet flavour. Ripened and stored in salted whey; best grilled or fried, and holds its shape well on being heated. Eat while still warm as it becomes tough and rubbery on cooling.
mozzarella soft, spun-curd cheese originating in southern Italy where it was traditionally made from water-buffalo milk. Now generally made from cow's milk, it is the most popular pizza cheese because of its low melting point and elasticity when heated.
parmesan also called parmigiano; is a hard, grainy cow-milk cheese originating in Italy. Reggiano is the best variety.
pizza cheese a commercial blend of varying proportions of processed grated mozzarella, cheddar and parmesan cheeses.
ricotta a soft, sweet, moist, white cow-milk cheese with a low fat content and a slightly grainy texture. The name roughly translates as 'cooked again' and refers to ricotta's manufacture from a whey that is itself a by-product of other cheese making.
CHICKEN
breast fillet breast halved, skinned and boned.
thigh skin and bone intact.
thigh cutlet thigh with skin and centre bone intact; sometimes found skinned with bone intact.
thigh fillet thigh with skin and centre bone removed.
CHICKPEAS (GARBANZO BEANS) also called hummus or channa; an irregularly round, sandy-coloured legume. Firm texture even after cooking, a floury mouth-feel and robust nutty flavour; available canned or dried (reconstitute for several hours in cold water before use).
CHILLI available in many types and sizes. Use rubber gloves when seeding and chopping fresh chillies as they can burn your skin. Removing membranes and seeds lessens the heat level.

glossary

flakes also sold as crushed chilli; dehydrated deep-red extremely fine slices and whole seeds.
green any unripened chilli; also some particular varieties that are ripe when green, such as jalapeño, habanero, poblano or serrano.
jalapeño pronounced hah-lah-pain-yo. Fairly hot, medium-sized, plump, dark green chilli; available pickled, canned or bottled, and fresh from greengrocers.
small red also known as thai or serrano; tiny, very hot and bright red in colour.
CHINESE FIVE SPICE a fragrant mixture of ground cinnamon, cloves, star anise, sichuan pepper and fennel seeds. Used in Chinese and other Asian cooking; available from most supermarkets or Asian food shops.
CHOCOLATE
choc bits also called chocolate chips or chocolate morsels; available in milk, white and dark chocolate. Made of cocoa liquor, cocoa butter, sugar and an emulsifier, these hold their shape in baking and are ideal for decorating.
dark (semi-sweet) also called luxury chocolate; made of a high percentage of cocoa liquor and cocoa butter, and little added sugar.
milk most popular eating chocolate, mild and very sweet; similar in make-up to dark chocolate with the difference being the addition of milk solids.
white contains no cocoa solids but derives its sweet flavour from cocoa butter. It is very sensitive to heat.
CHORIZO sausage of Spanish origin, made of coarsely ground pork and highly seasoned with garlic and chilli.
CINNAMON available in pieces (sticks or quills) and ground into powder; one of the world's most common spices, used as a sweet, fragrant flavouring for both sweet and savoury foods.
COCOA POWDER also known as unsweetened cocoa; cocoa beans (cacao seeds) that have been fermented, roasted, shelled, ground into powder then cleared of most of the fat content.
COCONUT
cream obtained commercially from the first pressing of the coconut flesh alone, without the addition of water; the second pressing (less rich) is sold as coconut milk. Available in cans and cartons at most supermarkets.
desiccated concentrated, dried, unsweetened and finely shredded coconut flesh.
CORNFLOUR (CORNSTARCH) available from corn (100% maize) or wheat (wheaten cornflour, gives a lighter texture in cakes); used as a thickening agent.

CORIANDER (CILANTRO) also called pak chee or chinese parsley; bright-green-leafed herb with a pungent flavour. Also available ground or as seeds; these should not be substituted for fresh coriander as the tastes are completely different.
CRANBERRIES available dried and frozen; have a rich, astringent flavour and can be used in cooking sweet and savoury dishes. The dried version can usually be substituted for or with other dried fruit.
CREAM
pouring also called pure or fresh cream; it contains no additives and a minimum fat content of 35%.
thick (double) a dolloping cream with a minimum fat content of 45%.
thickened (heavy) a whipping cream that contains a thickener. It has a minimum fat content of 35%.
CREAM OF TARTAR the acid ingredient in baking powder; added to confectionery mixtures to help prevent sugar from crystallising. Keeps frostings creamy and improves volume when beating egg whites.
CRÈME FRAÎCHE a mature, naturally fermented cream with a velvety texture and slightly tangy, nutty flavour. Minimum fat content 35%. A French variation of sour cream, it boils without curdling and is used in sweet and savoury dishes.
CUMIN also called zeera or comino; resembling caraway in size, cumin is the dried seed of a plant related to the parsley family. Available dried as seeds or ground, it has a spicy, almost curry-like flavour.
CURRY PASTES commercially prepared curry pastes vary in strength and flavour; use whichever one you feel best suits your spice-level tolerance.
DILL also known as dill weed; used fresh or dried, in seed form or ground. Its anise/celery sweetness flavours the food of the Scandinavian countries, and Germany and Greece. Its feathery, frond-like leaves are more subtle than the dried version or the seeds (which resemble caraway in flavour).
EGGS we use extra-large chicken eggs weighing an average of 60g each, unless stated otherwise.
EGGWASH beaten egg (white, yolk or both) and milk or water; often brushed over pastry or bread to impart colour or gloss.
FILLO PASTRY paper-thin sheets of raw pastry; brush each sheet with oil or melted butter, stack in layers, then cut and fold as directed.
FISH SAUCE also called nam pla or nuoc nam; made from pulverised salted fermented fish, most often anchovies. Has a pungent smell and strong taste, so use sparingly.

glossary

FLOUR
plain (all-purpose) unbleached wheat flour; is the best for baking as the gluten content ensures a strong dough for a light result.
self-raising all-purpose plain or wholemeal flour with baking powder and salt added; make at home in the proportion of 1 cup flour to 2 teaspoons baking powder.
wholemeal also called wholewheat flour; milled with the wheat germ so is higher in fibre and more nutritional than plain flour.
FOOD COLOURING vegetable-based substance available in liquid, paste or gel form.
FRUIT MINCE also known as mincemeat. A mix of fried fruits such as raisins, sultanas and candied peel, nuts, spices, apple, brandy or rum. It is used as a filling for cakes, puddings and fruit mince pies.
GARAM MASALA a blend of spices that includes cardamom, cinnamon, coriander, cloves, fennel and cumin. Black pepper and chilli can also be added for extra heat.
GINGER
fresh also called green or root ginger; thick gnarled root of a tropical plant.
ground also called powdered ginger; used as a flavouring in baking but cannot be substituted for fresh ginger.
HARISSA a North African paste made from dried red chillies, garlic, olive oil and caraway seeds; can be used as a rub for meats, an ingredient in sauces and dressings, or eaten as a condiment.
HAZELNUTS also known as filberts; plump, grape-sized, rich, sweet nut having a brown skin that is removed by rubbing heated nuts together vigorously in a tea-towel.
HOISIN SAUCE a thick, sweet and spicy Chinese barbecue sauce made from salted fermented soybeans, onions and garlic; used as a marinade or baste. Sold in supermarkets and Asian food shops.
HORSERADISH CREAM a commercially prepared creamy paste consisting of grated horseradish, vinegar, oil and sugar.
KAFFIR LIME LEAVES also known as bai magrood and looks like two glossy dark green leaves joined end to end, forming a rounded hourglass shape. Used fresh or dried in many South-East Asian dishes, they are used like bay leaves or curry leaves, especially in Thai cooking. Dried leaves are less potent so double the number you use if substituting for fresh; a strip of fresh lime peel may be substituted for each kaffir lime leaf.

MAPLE SYRUP, PURE distilled from the sap of sugar maple trees. Maple-flavoured syrup or pancake syrup is not an adequate substitute for the real thing.
MILK we use full-cream homogenised milk unless stated otherwise.
caramel top 'n' fill a canned milk product consisting of condensed milk that has been boiled to a caramel.
sweetened condensed a canned milk product consisting of milk with more than half the water content removed and sugar added to the remaining milk.
MIXED SPICE a classic spice mixture generally containing caraway, allspice, coriander, cumin, nutmeg and ginger, although cinnamon and other spices can be added. It is used with fruit and in cakes.
MUSHROOMS
flat large, flat mushrooms with an earthy flavour, ideal for filling and barbecuing. They are sometimes misnamed field mushrooms which are wild mushrooms.
portobello are mature, fully opened swiss browns; they are larger and bigger in flavour.
MUSTARD
dijon pale brown, distinctively flavoured, mild french mustard.
wholegrain also called seeded mustard. A French-style coarse-grain mustard made from crushed mustard seeds and Dijon-style french mustard.
NUTMEG a strong and pungent spice ground from the dried nut of an evergreen tree native to Indonesia. Usually found ground, the flavour is more intense from a whole nut, available from spice shops, so it's best to grate your own.
NUTRITIONAL YEAST a seasoning used to provide a moreish cheese-like umami taste, particularly for those on a vegan diet. Buy a brand that is fortified with B12, a vitamin required for development of healthy blood cells and the prevention of anaemia. Available from health food stores.
OIL
cooking spray we use a cholesterol-free cooking spray made from canola oil.
olive made from ripened olives. Extra virgin and virgin are the first and second press, respectively, of the olives and are therefore considered the best; the 'extra light' or 'light' name on other types refers to taste not fat levels.
peanut pressed from ground peanuts; most commonly used oil in Asian cooking because of its capacity to handle high heat without burning (high smoke point).
sesame used as a flavouring rather than for cooking.
vegetable oils sourced from plant fats.

glossary

ONIONS
green (scallions) also known, incorrectly, as shallots; an immature onion picked before the bulb has formed, having a long, bright-green edible stalk.
red also known as spanish, red spanish or bermuda onion; a sweet-flavoured, large, purple-red onion.
PAPRIKA ground dried sweet red capsicum (bell pepper); there are many grades and types available, including sweet, hot, mild and smoked.
PASTRY SHEETS ready-rolled packaged sheets of frozen puff and shortcrust pastry, available from supermarkets.
PROSCIUTTO a kind of unsmoked Italian ham; salted, air-cured and aged, it is usually eaten uncooked.
RHUBARB a plant with long, green-red stalks; becomes sweet and edible when cooked.
ROASTING/TOASTING desiccated coconut, pine nuts and sesame seeds roast more evenly if stirred over low heat in a heavy-based frying pan; their natural oils will help turn them golden. Remove from pan immediately. Nuts and dried coconut can be roasted in the oven to release their aromatic essential oils. Spread evenly onto an oven tray, roast at 180°C/350°F for about 5 minutes.
ROCKET (ARUGULA) also called rugula and rucola; peppery green leaf eaten raw in salads or in cooking. Baby rocket leaves are smaller and less peppery.
SESAME SEEDS black and white are the most common of this small oval seed, however there are also red and brown varieties. Used as an ingredient and as a condiment.
SOUR CREAM thick, commercially cultured sour cream with a minimum fat content of 35%.
SOY SAUCE made from fermented soya beans. Several varieties are available in supermarkets and Asian food stores. We use japanese soy sauce unless stated otherwise.
SPINACH also called english spinach and incorrectly, silver beet. Baby spinach leaves are eaten raw in salads or cooked until wilted.
SUGAR
brown very soft, finely granulated sugar retaining molasses for its characteristic colour and flavour.
caster (superfine) finely granulated table sugar.
icing (confectioners') also called powdered sugar; pulverised granulated sugar crushed with a little cornflour (cornstarch).
pure icing (confectioners') powdered sugar.

SUMAC a purple-red, astringent spice ground from berries that grow around the Mediterranean; adds a tart, lemony flavour to dips and dressings and goes well with barbecued meat.
TOMATOES
canned whole peeled tomatoes in natural juices; available crushed, chopped or diced. Use undrained.
paste triple-concentrated tomato puree used to flavour soups, stews and sauces.
puree canned pureed tomatoes (not tomato paste); substitute with fresh peeled and pureed tomatoes.
sauce (ketchup) a flavoured condiment made from tomatoes, vinegar and spices.
TURMERIC also called kamin; is a rhizome related to galangal and ginger. Known for the golden colour it imparts, fresh turmeric can be substituted with the more commonly found dried powder. When fresh turmeric is called for in a recipe, you can use dried powder instead.
VANILLA
bean dried, long, thin pod from a tropical golden orchid; the minuscule black seeds inside the bean are used to impart a luscious vanilla flavour in baking and desserts. A bean can be used three or four times.
extract made by extracting the flavour from the vanilla bean pod; pods are soaked, usually in alcohol, to capture the authentic flavour.
paste made from vanilla pods and contains real seeds. Is highly concentrated; 1 teaspoon replaces a whole vanilla pod. Available in most supermarkets in the baking section.
VINEGAR
rice wine a colourless vinegar made from fermented rice and flavoured with sugar and salt. Also known as seasoned rice vinegar; sherry can be substituted.
white made from distilled grain alcohol.
WASABI also called wasabe; an Asian horseradish used to make the pungent, green-coloured sauce traditionally served with Japanese raw fish dishes; sold in powdered or paste form.
WORCESTERSHIRE SAUCE thin, dark-brown spicy sauce developed by the British when in India; used as a seasoning for meat, gravies and cocktails, and as a condiment.
YOGHURT we use plain full-cream yoghurt unless noted otherwise.
greek plain yoghurt that has been strained in a cloth (muslin) to remove the whey and to give it a creamy consistency.
ZUCCHINI also called courgette; small, pale- or dark-green or yellow vegetable of the squash family.

CONVERSION CHART

MEASURES

One Australian metric measuring cup holds approximately 250ml; one Australian metric tablespoon holds 20ml; one Australian metric teaspoon holds 5ml. The difference between one country's measuring cups and another's is within a two- or three-teaspoon variance and will not affect your cooking results. North America, New Zealand and the United Kingdom use a 15ml tablespoon. All cup and spoon measurements are level.

The most accurate way of measuring dry ingredients is to weigh them.

When measuring liquids, use a clear glass or plastic jug with the metric markings.

We use extra-large eggs with an average weight of 60g.

OVEN TEMPERATURES

The oven temperatures in this book are for conventional and fan-forced ovens.

	°C (Celsius)	°F (Fahrenheit)
Very slow	120	250
Slow	150	300
Moderately slow	160	325
Moderate	180	350
Moderately hot	200	400
Hot	220	425
Very hot	240	475

DRY MEASURES

metric	imperial
15g	½oz
30g	1oz
60g	2oz
90g	3oz
125g	4oz (¼lb)
155g	5oz
185g	6oz
220g	7oz
250g	8oz (½lb)
280g	9oz
315g	10oz
345g	11oz
375g	12oz (¾lb)
410g	13oz
440g	14oz
470g	15oz
500g	16oz (1lb)
750g	24oz (1½lb)
1kg	32oz (2lb)

LIQUID MEASURES

metric	imperial
30ml	1 fluid oz
60ml	2 fluid oz
100ml	3 fluid oz
125ml	4 fluid oz
150ml	5 fluid oz
190ml	6 fluid oz
250ml	8 fluid oz
300ml	10 fluid oz
500ml	16 fluid oz
600ml	20 fluid oz
1000ml (1 litre)	1¾ pints

LENGTH MEASURES

metric	imperial
3mm	⅛in
6mm	¼in
1cm	½in
2cm	¾in
2.5cm	1in
5cm	2in
6cm	2½in
8cm	3in
10cm	4in
13cm	5in
15cm	6in
18cm	7in
20cm	8in
22cm	9in
25cm	10in
28cm	11in
30cm	12in (1ft)

INDEX

A

apples
   easy apple pies 52
   pork, sage & apple pies 40
apricot danishes 63
asian fish cakes with chilli-mayo
   dipping sauce 172
aussie meat pies 25
avocado
   cream 155
   guacamole 47

B

bachelor's big breakfast 167
bacon & egg pies 14
bananas
   banana bread muffins 129
   banoffee pies 93
banoffee pies 93
beef
   aussie meat pies 25
   beef shiraz pies 29
   beef taco pies 21
   cheeseburger pies 148
   lasagne 144
   pub-style Guinness
      beef pies 26
   sausage rolls 147
   spaghetti bolognese
      muffins 151
berries
   any berry pies 55
   berry custard croissant
      puddings 130
   pikelets with raspberries &
      crème fraîche 107
   raspberry & frangipane tarts
      60
   strawberry rhubarb
      crumble pies 56

big 'the works' pizza 159
breakfast, bachelor's big 167
brownies, triple choc-chunk 125
butter chicken roti pies 43

C

cakes
   carrot 119
   chocolate cupcakes &
      strawberry buttercream 126
   chocolate lava 115
   eight-layer celebration 141
   lemonade jelly 116
   victoria sponge 120
caramel
   banoffee pies 93
   caramel pecan pies 82
   chocolate fudge caramel
      tarts 85
carrot cakes 119
cartwheels 81
cauliflower cheeze pies, vegan
   22
cheat's
   béchamel 144
   lemon meringue pies 67
cheese
   mac 'n' cheese 175
   spinach & three cheese
      muffins 179
cheeseburger pies 148
cheesecake, baked lemon
   mango 112
cherries
   black forest pie 89
   cherry lattice pies 59
chicken
   butter chicken roti pies 43
   chicken quesadillas with
      avocado cream 155

(*chicken* continued)
   smoky chicken & corn pies
      10
   thai chicken curry pies 30
chocolate
   black forest pie 89
   cartwheels 81
   choc-peanut butter brownie
      pies 90
   chocolate cookies 96
   chocolate cupcakes &
      strawberry buttercream 126
   chocolate fudge caramel
      tarts 85
   chocolate lava cakes 115
   easy-as-pie ice-cream
      sandwiches 104
   eight-layer celebration
      cake 141
   lamingtons 111
   mississippi mud pies 86
   s'mores 99
   triple choc-chunk brownies 125
cinnamon scrolls 108
coconut & passionfruit
   impossible pies 71
cookies
   chocolate 96
   easy cookies & cream pies 74
corn
   fritters 180
   smoky chicken & corn pies 10
curry pies
   butter chicken roti pies 43
   lamb korma 36
   thai chicken 30
custard 130
   berry custard croissant
      puddings 130
   classic custard tarts 68

index

D
danishes, apricot 63
date puddings, sticky 133
doughnuts
   funfetti doughnuts 103
   jam doughnuts 100

E
easy cookies & cream pies 74
eggs
   bachelor's big breakfast 167
   bacon & egg pies 14
   prosciutto egg cups 163

F
fish
   asian fish cakes with chilli-mayo dipping sauce 172
   fish mornay & potato pies 44
   smoked ocean trout & wasabi pies 17
frangipane 60
fritters, corn 180
fruit mince pies 64
funfetti doughnuts 103

G
guacamole 47
Guinness beef pies, pub-style 26

H
haloumi
   haloumi, harissa & honey brioche sliders 182
   lamb kofta & haloumi wraps 152
ham & pineapple mini pizzas 156
hot cross bun scones 137
hot dogs, mini 164

I
ice-cream sandwiches, easy-as-pie 104

J
jackfruit pies, pulled with asian slaw 48
jam doughnuts 100
jelly cakes, lemonade 116

L
lamb
   lamb kofta & haloumi wraps 152
   lamb korma pies 36
   moroccan lamb pies 33
   shepherd's pies 39
lamingtons 111
lasagne 144
lattice pies, cherry 59
lemonade jelly cakes 116
lemons
   baked lemon mango cheesecake 112
   cheat's lemon meringue pies 67
lime pies, key 78

M
mac 'n' cheese 175
mango
   baked lemon mango cheesecake 112
meringue
   cheat's lemon meringue pies 67
   mini pavlovas 138
mississippi mud pies 86
moroccan lamb pies 33
muffins
   banana bread 129
   spaghetti bolognese 151
   spinach & three cheese 179
mushroom pies 18

N
nachos pie, vegetarian 47
Nutella scrolls 108
nuts
   caramel pecan pies 82
   raspberry & frangipane tarts 60

O
ocean trout, smoked & wasabi pies 17

P
passionfruit
   coconut & passionfruit impossible pies 71
pavlovas, mini 138
peaches & cream pies 77
peanut butter
   choc-peanut butter brownie pies 90
pecans
   caramel pecan pies 82
pikelets with raspberries & crème fraîche 107
pizzas
   big 'the works' pizza 159

index

(*pizzas* continued)
   ham & pineapple mini 156
   pizza scrolls 160
pork
   pork, sage & apple pies 40
   sausage rolls 147
potatoes
   fish mornay & potato pies 44
prosciutto egg cups 163
pub-style Guinness beef pies 26
puddings
   berry custard croissant 130
   sticky date 133

Q

quesadillas, chicken with
   avocado cream 155
quiches, spring 176

R

raspberries
   pikelets with raspberries &
     crème fraîche 107
   raspberry & frangipane tarts
     60
reuben toastie 168
rhubarb
   strawberry rhubarb crumble
     pies 56
russian dressing 168

S

sauces
   cheat's béchamel 144
   cheeze 22
   chilli-mayo dipping 172
sausage rolls 147
savoury pies
   aussie meat 25
   bacon & egg 14

(*savoury pies* continued)
   beef shiraz 29
   beef taco 21
   butter chicken roti 43
   cheeseburger 148
   fish mornay & potato 44
   lamb korma 36
   moroccan lamb 33
   mushroom 18
   pub-style Guinness beef 26
   pulled jackfruit pies with
     asian slaw 48
   pork, sage & apple 40
   shepherd's 39
   smoked ocean trout &
     wasabi 17
   smoky chicken & corn 10
   thai chicken curry 30
   turkey & cranberry 13
   vegan cauliflower cheeze 22
   vegetarian nachos 47
scones 134
   hot cross bun scones 137
scrolls
   cinnamon 108
   Nutella 108
   pizza 160
shepherd's pies 39
sliders, haloumi, harissa &
   honey brioche 182
s'mores 99
spaghetti bolognese muffins 151
spinach
   big spinach cob 171
   spinach & three cheese
     muffins 179
spring quiches 176
sticky date puddings 133
strawberries
   chocolate cupcakes &
     strawberry buttercream 126

(*strawberries* continued)
   strawberry rhubarb
     crumble pies 56
sweet pies
   any berry 55
   banoffee 93
   black forest 89
   caramel pecan 82
   cheat's lemon meringue 67
   cherry lattice 59
   choc-peanut butter brownie 90
   coconut & passionfruit
     impossible 71
   easy apple 52
   easy cookies & cream 74
   fruit mince 64
   key lime 78
   mississippi mud 86
   strawberry rhubarb
     crumble pies 56

T

taco pies, beef 21
tarts
   chocolate fudge caramel 85
   classic custard 68
   raspberry & frangipane 60
thai chicken curry pies 30
toastie, reuben 168
turkey & cranberry pies 13

V

vegan cauliflower cheeze pies 22
vegetarian nachos pie 47
victoria sponge 120

W

wasabi
   smoked ocean trout &
     wasabi pies 17

Published in 2020 by Bauer Media Books, Australia.
Bauer Media Books is a division of Bauer Media Pty Ltd.

BAUER MEDIA GROUP
Chief executive officer
Brendon Hill
Chief financial officer
Andrew Stedwell

BAUER MEDIA BOOKS
Publisher
Sally Eagle
Editorial & food director
Sophia Young
Creative director & designer
Hannah Blackmore
Managing editor
Stephanie Kistner
Food editor
Sophia Young
Operations manager
David Scotto
Business development manager
Simone Aquilina
saquilina@bauer-media.com.au
Ph +61 2 8268 6278

Photographer & Stylist Bree Hutchins
Photochef Bree Hutchins
Recipe development Bree Hutchins
Assistant photochef & stylist assistant
Katherine Hunt
Hand model Michelle Gauntlett

Cover & additional pages
Photographer Con Poulos
Stylist Olivia Blackmore
Photochef Vikki Moursellas

Printed in China by
1010 Printing International

A catalogue record for this book
is available from the National
Library of Australia.
ISBN 978-1-92586-505-9

© Bauer Media Pty Limited 2020
ABN 18 053 273 546

This publication is copyright.
No part of it may be reproduced
or transmitted in any form
without the written permission
of the publisher.

Published by Bauer Media Books,
a division of Bauer Media Pty Ltd,
54 Park St, Sydney; GPO Box 4088,
Sydney, NSW 2001, Australia
Ph +61 2 8116 9334;
Fax +61 2 9126 3702
www.awwcookbooks.com.au

International rights manager
Simone Aquilina
saquilina@bauer-media.com.au
Ph +61 2 8268 6278

Order books
phone 136 116 (within Australia)
or order online at
www.awwcookbooks.com.au
Send recipe enquiries to
recipeenquiries@bauer-media.com.au

 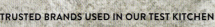